INTERPRETIVE ADVENTURES

INTERPRETIVE ADVENTURES
SUBVERSIVE READINGS IN A MISSIONAL SCHOOL

The following is a collection of
the types of readings taught to my students at
Global Outreach Developments International (G.O.D.).

PHILLIP MICHAEL GARNER

WIPF & STOCK · Eugene, Oregon

INTERPRETIVE ADVENTURES
Subversive Readings in a Missional School

Copyright © 2017 Mike Garner. All rights reserved. Except for brief quotations in critical publications or reviews, no part of this book may be reproduced in any manner without prior written permission from the publisher. Write: Permissions, Wipf and Stock Publishers, 199 W. 8th Ave., Suite 3, Eugene, OR 97401.

Wipf & Stock
An Imprint of Wipf and Stock Publishers
199 W. 8th Ave., Suite 3
Eugene, OR 97401

www.wipfandstock.com

PAPERBACK ISBN: 978-1-5326-1827-7
HARDCOVER ISBN: 978-1-4982-4370-4

Manufactured in the U.S.A.   MAY 4, 2017

Dedication

I want to thank my students for whom I have written this book, and my parents Darrell and Gerrie for their encouragement. My son Gregg for believing I have something to offer to the learning community, and the young people of G.O.D. International that embraced my teaching. I also want to acknowledge the graciousness of Paul Alexander for his support.

PREFACE

THE BIBLICAL THEOLOGICAL AND SPIRITUAL DEVELOPMENT OF A CHRISTIAN COMMUNITY

The following pages are teachings that represent the spiritual and theological groundings that contributed to the development of a Christian community named Global Outreach Developments International. My role in this community was multifaceted, although it was primarily to serve as the Dean and Director of the missionary training institute. This is not a narrative history of the movements birthing and development. I will leave the task of producing a historical narrative of the beginnings and growth to others. The following chapters and their contents contain a brief but accurate unfolding of theology which my students were taught in the process of becoming educated under the guidance of the school's curricular design and the ministry's overall practice. The movement's corporate identity is Global Outreach Developments International (G.O.D. International). G.O.D. International is a community of believers that seeks to transplant communities in various nations of the world through a liberative theological and communal practice. The varied nuances of the use of the word liberative include the spiritual liberation gained through relationship with Christ, liberation from the crippling effects brought on by lack of education, and a non- violent approach to social change through the moral force of presence and the challenging of injustice through the use of media for public awareness. My task has been to develop a program of study that would produce in the students a depth of spirituality that would enable them to face the many challenges of countering the nationalistic, denominational, and paternalistic missional practices of the past with a theologically driven paradigm, which I hope will bring about change on a social, cultural, and religious level. Explaining the application of these theologically driven practices is not the primary aim of the following chapters; such a task would require another book. My interpretive offerings are often unique perspectives and are not reworked productions from the writings of others. Nonetheless, my growth as a student of the biblical text has benefited immensely from the writings of others. The following, then, is not just a theology but a record of key biblical texts and original interpretations that have contributed to my own reading of the Bible and produced a theological view of the world which empowered me to teach the people that make up the community of G.O.D. International. I suggest that if you are not familiar with the biblical passages to which I refer, read with your Bible in hand. Although I draw upon a variety of resources, the Bible is central to the theological and spiritual development of Christian community, just as is the gracious presence and work of God's spirit.

Table of Contents

Preface vii

1. Spiritual Exemplarship 1
   Re-Establishing Metaphor 2
   Spirituality or Symbols 7
   Israel's First Singular Symbol 9
   Spirituality as Theological Practice 11
   Spiritual Authority 11
   Stories and the Spiritual Development of
   the G.O.D. International Community 14
       Spiritual Development and Character 16
       A New Narrative and Character Development 16
       Character and Testing 17
       Character and Education 17
       Character and Academics 18
   A Model for Developing a Spiritual Community 19

2. Acceptable Worship 23
   Living Is Greater Than Ritual 24
   Creativity and Nonviolence: From Ritual to Maturity 28
   An Etiology for Ritual Sacrifice as
   an Anthropological Phenomenon 32
   Called Alongside: The Church's Position in the World 36
   A Nonviolent God 38
   In Harm's Way 38
   Conclusion 41

3. The Art of Subversive Narrative Storytelling 43
   The Function of Subversive Storytelling 45
   Reading Biblical Stories as Subversive Art 46
       1 Kings 3:16-28 - A Story Of Wisdom? 46

      Acts 4:32–5:16 - Great Grace, Great Power,
      and Great Fear 48
  Spiritual Stories and the Deconstruction
  of Historical Myths 50
      Suspicious of the Powers 50
      2 Samuel 2:11-17 - Old Warriors and Dead Heroes 50
  The Spiritual Quest to Locate God in History 52
      Hide and Seek 52
      2 Samuel 5:22-25 - Thus Says 'Who'? 53
  When God Liberates, Look for Mercy 54
      An Interpretive Lens for Reading 54
      Mercy amidst Plagues 56
      Yhwh Forced to Assert His Right over Life 60
      Yhwh Reigns and War is Madness 62
  Conclusion 63

4. A Feminist Study of the Female Characters
    Portrayed in Judges 65
    Immoral Structures of Oppression 66
    Reading Judges as a Study on the Declension
    of the Female Voice 69
      Achsah the Vociferous Woman, Judges 1:12-15 69
      Deborah the Prophetess of Peace, Judges 4 and 5 70
      Jael the Female Assassin, Judges 4:17-22 71
      An Unknown Woman Saves a City, Judges 9:50 – 57 73
      The Righteous Daughter of Brash Words, Judges 11 75
      Yhwh Speaks to a Barren Woman, Judges 13 77
      A Strong Man, a Submissive Woman,
      and a Prostitute, Judges 14-16:3 78
      Delilah: Loved but Unloving, Judges 16:4-31 78
      Religion, Greed, and Israel's Widows, Judges 17 78
      The Silent Concubine, Judges 19 79
    Conclusion 82

5. Interpretive Adventures in a Christian Community
    a Conceptual Introduction 85
    Not All Texts Are Equal 87
      Primary Texts and Political Readings 88
      The Bible and the Reader 89
    Theology and Revelation 90
      Revelation Liberates Humanity 91
      Inward Liberation 92

    Restoring the Voice of Oppressed Communities............93
        Theological Education and Liberation............93
        A Lived Kerygma for Communities
        of Need in the Philippines............93
        Proclamation and Practice among Endangered Guardians............94
        Bringing Christ to Endangered Guardians in the Bars............96
        Proclamation and Practice in Hope's Refuge............98
        Proclamation and Practice with Prisons and Families............100
        Born Free: The Right of Tribal People
        to Live Unmolested............101
        Exploited Labor............102
    Conclusion............102

6. Spiritual Formation in Community: Church
    Renewal and the Role of Character............105
    Introduction............105
    Renewal............107
    Spirituality............111
    Jeremiah: A Case Study in Spiritual Formation............112
    Hope's Indomitable Struggle............117
    A Short Story on Character............118
    An Alternative Community............119

Bibliography............121

CHAPTER 1
SPIRITUAL EXEMPLARSHIP

In this first chapter my effort is to offer a biblically supported theology for understanding Christian leadership. I will begin by re-establishing the metaphor of the new birth. I offer this teaching to my students as a basic beginning to an assortment of new perspectives for interpreting biblical texts. It is my opinion that one of the current weak points of Christian spiritual practice lies in its failure to revisit established metaphors and symbols for the depth of meaning beyond popular views. For instance, the new birth metaphor is valuable for Christian instruction and needs to be interpreted in light of spiritual formation, not as a finished confessional experience for the seeker.

Within the religious community the social construction of symbols is used to maintain the status of the religious powers. The deconstruction of symbols is imperative for spiritual development. This is so because the meaning of a symbol is always more important than the symbol. The lessons of the Bible on the power of symbol are like a theological stream of thought that flows throughout the canon. I utilize the story of the first 'ark' according to the instruction of Deuteronomy. I will further affirm the theological deconstruction of the ark as symbol utilizing both books of Samuel and the book of Jeremiah.[1]

I offer a brief section on *spiritual authority*, which is presented within the Bible as the work of God existing outside of political and religious systems that maintain their power through titles and symbols. I will contend that to recognize spiritual authority is to affirm that which God has already confirmed. Writing from a Judeo-Christian perspective, I believe it is evident that those prophetic and

---

[1] The complete dismantling of Israel's symbolic world and the repudiation of ritual is portrayed in the book of Jeremiah with unequaled clarity in relation to the rest of the Old Testament.

apostolic personalities who have borne spiritual authority were without authority in the sphere of institutional structures.

I will address the believer's spiritual need for stories and argue that they are points of departure for spiritual interpretation. The importance of stories is made evident by the use of the unfolding drama of biblical revelation within the family of Abraham. The recognition of our role in forming the ongoing story of history is essential for the development of a community. I will share the spiritual practices and development of the community in which I lived and served.

I will conclude with a model for developing a spiritual community that seeks to regain the loss of metaphorical meaning and be free from the constraining power of symbols in both form and language. I will describe a community that seeks to resist systemic institutional powers that would ignore spiritual authority embodied in a person that is a living examplar of spirituality.

Re-Establishing Metaphor

Metaphors are a common literary device in scripture. Metaphors communicate to us through words and pictures. Although the interpreter must discipline the imagination to employ the metaphor within the boundaries of its intended use, the imagination is essential for interpretation. All metaphors used in scripture breakdown if they are analyzed beyond their literary and theological intent. Time and consistent employing of a metaphor to support confessional statements corrupt the meaning of a metaphor.[2] So, metaphors must be revisited for the purpose of reestablishing their status as metaphor. Over time metaphors lose their meaning, become a symbol, and their educational role is lost to a failure of imagination.[3] A metaphor that has become a symbol no longer stimulates the imagination. The result is that the transcendent power of the divine spirit to inspire the human spirit and imagination is replaced with a naive reading that produces

---

[2] Confessional statements are generally pedagogic and lack depth of thought unless they are followed with much explanation. A brief confessional statement is not meant to communicate complexity of meaning. Confessional statements limit the imaginative use of language by controlling the meaning of metaphors and symbols. Imagination is essential for drawing the transcendent reality into our false reality.

[3] An obvious example is the worship of Jesus' blood in song and ritual. The blood of Jesus is a metaphorical way of representing his life. Abel's blood did not literally cry out to God; rather, the loss of life was understood to be represented by the blood that returned to the earth (life-sustaining, red, blood). Leviticus also attests to the life represented in the blood (Lev. 17:14).

structures of thought limited to simplistic symbolic inference.[4] At this point the symbol determines the meaning because the symbol becomes more important than the meaning.

The popularity of the new birth metaphor in John 3 is an example of confessional usage that confines the work of the spirit to the limitations placed upon language by religious powers. The passage serves multiple theological purposes. I will focus on two of the major lessons. One of the purposes of John is to establish the term 'eternal life' as an equivalent for 'kingdom of God.' The passage opens with Nicodemus acknowledging that the 'presence of God' is with Jesus; else he could not perform the 'signs.' In response to Nicodemus' positive statement Jesus' answer seems to confirm Nicodemus' own state; he is close to entering the kingdom. Nicodemus has acknowledged that Jesus is a teacher, and that the presence of God is with him. Jesus equates the 'presence of God' with the 'kingdom of God.'

In the gospel of John the phrase 'Kingdom of God' is found twice. Both instances are found in the third chapter of John during Jesus' night-time encounter with the Pharisee Nicodemus. The final line of this particular pericope (verses 1-15) reads that whoever believes in him may have 'eternal life.'[5] Jesus' first words are about the kingdom, and his last are about eternal life. To enter the kingdom is to possess eternal life. Thus John transitions use of the potentially dangerous idea of 'kingdom' into the existential idea of 'eternal life'. Eternal life in John is something that is now present for all who will enter the Kingdom of God, making the two phrases synonymous, yet a

---

[4] The transcendent is sought from our earthbound position, but is met in the prophetic imagination that seeks the reign of God in the present on the earth. Further, the meaning behind a symbol is always more important than the symbol. Political, religious, and national symbols distort meaning and represent an ideal that is placed upon the symbol by those who control thought. A symbol cannot produce the meaning it carries; it can only deceive. Symbols produce a false unity of collective consciousness that fails to question the propagandist's inability to manifest the ideal. The phrase 'born again' has been reduced to a symbol and a confession; it has lost its meaning across the globe due to the political power of western Christianity.

[5] I contend that John 3:1-15 forms a distinct literary unit. Verses 16-21 of chapter 3 reflect the theological teaching of the community and are a response to their rejection and persecution by the synagogues. Verse 15 brings closure to Jesus' answer of Nicodemus' question in verse 10. Further, the general tenor of the text changes at verse 16 from answer to commentary. The influence of the Johannine community upon this text is affirmed in the 'we' of verse 11; unless Jesus' is speaking in concert with the prophetic teachers of Israel, Nicodemus' has identified Jesus as a teacher come from God.

varied nuance is present in the transaction of terms.⁶ One of the reasons for the change is found in Jesus' words.

> Jesus answered, "My kingdom is not from this world. If my kingdom were from this world, my followers would be fighting to keep me from being handed over to the Jews. But as it is, my kingdom is not from here"⁷ (John 18:36, NRSV).

Although Jesus' Kingdom is not of this world, it is present and can be discerned through the 'sign' that is Jesus. The identification of Jesus' origin as 'from God' is spoken by both Nicodemus and Jesus. Nicodemus lies at the threshold of the kingdom and of receiving eternal life (transformation through conformation to the image of God in Christ); he need only believe in the ongoing work of Christ. The work of Christ culminates in his death and resurrection (verses 14 and 15). Jesus' response to Nicodemus is recorded in John 3:3 ("Jesus answered him, 'Very truly, I tell you, no one can see the kingdom of God without being born from above.'") The visionary world of the prophets has begun and is manifested in the human heart of those that are spiritual.

Nicodemus' response (John 3:4, "'How can anyone be born after having grown old? Can one enter a second time into the mother's womb and be born?'") is the pedagogical understanding of the metaphor that is used by the writer to communicate the birth from above. Jesus does not discredit the validity of Nicodemus' question, but allows his question in all of its absurdity to stand as a credible response. Nicodemus' response now serves as one of the movements necessary for grasping Jesus' teaching on 'seeing' 'the kingdom of God'; that is, on the reception of 'eternal life'. Jesus' response in verse five has the reader 'entering' the kingdom of God, rather than being able to 'see'. Further, Jesus' response is enigmatic. For how are we to understand a birth that is of the Spirit, a birth that is unseen like the wind, yet powerful like the wind? It is Nicodemus' question that places the metaphor of physical birth as a springboard for understanding.

Jesus' response in verse three comes from his mouth without any inquiry or question posed from Nicodemus. The issue is the Kingdom of God, and Jesus knows what Nicodemus really needs to talk about. Jesus informs Nicodemus that the Kingdom is an unseen reality that can be seen only by persons gifted with

---

⁶ The term eternal life is descriptive of the breaking in of God's reality through the people of God or the body of Christ. Eternal life is used to signify the beginning transformation of the world through the transformation of human beings.

⁷ The nonviolent nature of Jesus' kingdom will not allow for its comparison with Caesar's kingdom. The use of eternal life is as a replacement phrase for the common political meaning of 'basileia' (kingdom). It is a change of language and safer for the Johannine community in their politically charged environment.

the ability to see through an act of God equivalent to being born. Nicodemus' questions focus on the word 'born'. When we are born, life has just begun; we make our entrance as infants without understanding or power. As a leader and teacher, Nicodemus possesses both understanding and power. However, it is the weakness and failure of Nicodemus' life that will follow him into this new world that Jesus has invited him to enter. Nicodemus cannot hide behind titles and institutional authority. Nicodemus seeks further explanation upon the idea of birth in relation to seeing the Kingdom (verses five and six form Jesus' answer). Nicodemus must experience the life-giving power of God in a manner that opens his eyes to see what he has never seen before. Standing before Nicodemus is the King of the Kingdom; that is, the son of man or the son of God revealed in humanness.

In order to see and enter, Nicodemus will have to find God in a human being. It is the image of God in every human being that is revelatory of God, and this is particularly so in Jesus.[8] Until Nicodemus lets go of his worldly power and learns to live as 'spirit' and function on a basis of 'spiritual authority' over his institutionally ordained power, he will remain disconnected from the reign of God. The greatest must learn to serve from a position of equality rather than symbolically maintained authority.

The Kingdom has entered and continues to enter the present world through an unseen power that is not found in the world's institutions, societies, or cultures. Persons born of the 'Spirit' are empowered with a strength that is not recognized within human constructs, yet is as natural as the wind itself. Persons born of the Spirit see the Kingdom and possess a power that cannot be domesticated or controlled. The Kingdom of God has entered the world and cannot be isolated to the nation of Israel. The Kingdom of God belongs to all persons who receive the gift of life found in the person of Jesus, the 'son of man', who saves the world with an act of love while simultaneously condemning the world systems that legitimate his death.

The present possession of eternal life is now the sign of entering the Kingdom of God. Jesus is now the object of faith that opens the eyes and enables people to see the Kingdom of God. Entrance into the Kingdom is a radical experience with

---

[8] Loving God must first be done by loving human beings who reveal God through the image of God which they bear. The image of God is carried by all human beings, yet is not seen as it should be due to their failure to reach the maturity of spirit that is manifest in Jesus. It must also be kept in mind that the Johannine community is writing their gospel after the death and resurrection of Jesus. The accomplished life of Jesus is portrayed to the readers, including knowledge of his resurrection, and this affects the readers' perception of the message beyond any historical moment between Nicodemus and Jesus. Colossians states that Jesus is the image of the invisible God.

God brought about by recognizing and receiving the 'signs' in the life of Jesus, which include the cross and the eternal life that culminates in resurrection.

Birth is a traumatic event, an event that all of us have experienced. From the warmth of our mother's womb we emerge into this world. We enter this life from a place of resting, a liquid world where all our needs are met by the one that carries us. Suddenly our liquid-filled chamber breaks and muscles contract, and we find ourselves being pushed out an opening that seems too small for our passing. Entering this life, we pass from comfort to discomfort, and complete trauma becomes the order of the day. When we make our appearance into this life, our eyes are exposed to light for the first time, our lungs demand that we breathe, and our food line is severed before we even finish crying.

The metaphor of birth is first presented by Jesus as 'born from above'. Jesus himself relates the experience to the trauma of birth. When we are born from above, it is a traumatic experience because for the first time we see the world through the eyes of the Spirit. For the first time the vanity of the present world pales in contrast to the presence of God that fills our newfound lungs. This entrance into the kingdom of God, this reception of eternal life, has placed us into a new world of possibilities. For the first time we see, breathe, and must learn to eat; there is no desire to return to the womb.

The 'new birth' opens our eyes to a world of injustice, of vanity, a world where God's will is not done, and God himself is replaced with idols of militarism, materialism, national security, personal security, and self-righteous religious belief.[9] The 'new birth' also opens our eyes to see the kingdom and to demonstrate the presence of the kingdom in the now. The 'new birth' places us in a kingdom where humanity learns to live together without war and without greed. As a citizen of such a kingdom, I find myself living in a constructed world, a false reality, an untruth, which has lost its appeal. Possessing eternal life, the believer is capable of experiencing a power that delivers him/her from the fear of death. When we enter the King's kingdom, we begin to possess the heart of the King because he has given us his Spirit. The King saw this world as a place in need of

---

[9] It has been my observation that most American Christians are guilty of idolatry in relation to the idol of militarism. Most, if not all, have been grateful for the sense of safety they enjoy in spite of the danger of nuclear obliteration and the injustices perpetrated around the world by our militarily enforced economic interests. This also leads to accepting the idolatry of materialism, which permeates both church and society. I would think that this acceptance of militarism and materialism is followed by a sense of ethnocentrism which is inconsistent with the oneness of humanity taught throughout the Bible.

his light and life. The King came to set the captive free and bring good news to the poor. The King refuses to be a king; he follows Deuteronomy 17's injunctions.[10]

The business of appropriation and accumulation belongs to the world, whereas the business of the Kingdom is the establishment of peace, of self-sacrifice, of giving our lives as Jesus gave his. This 'new birth' is not so we can secure our reserved seat in heaven; it is so that we can be children of God in the present, filled with his Spirit and growing in the knowledge of his love and grace. The power who now resides in the person that is 'born from above' is the presence of God. The person who is born from above is to become the 'sign' that God's reign is present. The person born from above has a heart like the king and lives to die for the lost. We are to be a people who die daily to the luring claims of greatness offered by the world and at the same time refuse ever to kill for the sake of preserving our beliefs.

The new birth is not to be reduced to an immediate experience where a person is born fully matured. The new birth metaphor plays out over the lives of all believers until the day we all arrive at maturity in Christ. The lifelong traumatic challenge to pick up our cross and follow Jesus brings about spiritual formation that evidences the power of eternal life. The eternal life we possess is expressed through a people that are free from the fear of death. As part of Chrisitian witness, the 'art of dying' is as important as birth and living.

Spirituality or Symbols

Israel's initial symbol is rich with meaning but is eventually abandoned because the symbol became more important than the meaning. The meaning of a symbol is always more important than the symbol. The Israelites' initial symbol identifying them with God is circumcision. This symbol of circumcision is given to Abraham in Genesis 17. Circumcision is present individually in the flesh of each male, whereas the symbol of the ark is singular and external to all Israel.

The meaning of circumcision is easily connected to several aspects of the biblical text and human biology. First, Abraham is promised that his seed will fill the earth. In Genesis 18:19, the writer clarifies the task of Abraham in regard to his

---

[10] Deuteronomy 17:14-20 allows for Israel to have a king; however, the requirements for the king prohibit him from ever being a king. The term 'king' must take on new meaning when applied to Jesus. Jesus reigns victorious over human existence and opens the heavens. He is a nonviolent king who calls us friends, and the humanity of God is revealed in him as is the image of God. Conformation of a human being into the image of God revealed in Christ is the work of God in the world. We are to participate in this work by teaching and living as exemplars.

progeny (seed). Abraham is to charge his children to keep the way of Yhwh, which is to do righteousness and justice. This charge is corollary with God's command for Israel to teach her children the meaning of God's revelation amidst the history of Israel, particularly their deliverance from Egypt.

The male Israelite carried in his person, cut in his genitals, the sign, or seal of the covenant that God made with Abraham as a perpetual practice. They were to be like their father and teach their children after them. In part, the story of Judah, his erring sons, and Tamar, sits in contrast to God's expectations for male Israelite behavior. Male Israelites were to guard their 'seed'; they were to control their sexual desires and be responsible as males to teach their children righteousness and justice. Circumcision in the male Israelite indicated that men were to govern over their sexual impulses responsibly, and that men are able to do so. The seed of the Israelite male belonged to God, therefore the sexual behavior of the Israelite male was to represent self-control, righteousness, and justice. The meaning of the cutting represented the claim that males could control their sexual impulse. For example, Hosea's writing holds males responsible for the sexual behavior of women in society (Hosea 4:14).[11]

I understand the Bible to teach us that males have more control over their sexuality than women.[12] Men are takers, and women are givers. Women lose their virginity, while men lose nothing. Women bleed monthly and are reminded of the potential for life, and menopause sets a limit on their reproductive years. The Israelite male's cutting in the flesh was to serve as a reminder that their sexuality and seed belonged to God. The meaning is more important than the symbol

---

[11] Hosea 4:14: "I will not punish your daughters when they play the whore, nor your daughters-in-law when they commit adultery; for the men themselves go aside with whores, and sacrifice with temple prostitutes; thus a people without understanding comes to ruin." The declaration that God will not punish the daughters nor the daughters-in-law is because the men are guilty of insuring that the societal structures that promote the immoral behavior of women exist. These social structures cannot function without the approval and participation of the men.

[12] Both scripture and nature teach that women are more sensual than men. However, their sensuality can contribute to spiritual development because the more sensuous, the more need to become spirit. The less sensuous male has greater control over sensuousness (sexuality). Paul uses a similar argument in 1 Corinthians 11:13-16. Paul associates sensuality and women with the glory or covering of long hair. See Soren Kierkegaard, *The Concept of Anxiety*, trans. Thomte and Anderson (Princeton: Princeton University Press, 1980), 49, 69, 86, 92, 190, 246.

or sign of circumcision. This is why circumcision can be abandoned; it is only a symbol or sign.[13]

Israel's First Singular Symbol

Israel's first singular symbol for all of the people marks a definitive change in the use of symbolism because the symbol is not personal, not cut in the flesh, and its meaning represents Israel's failure. This symbol is the original 'ark', or box, built by Moses when he was on the mountain with God. Moses is on the mountain (Deut. 10:1), and God has Moses build an ark to contain the two stone tablets of the Decalogue. This is the set of tablets which Moses made after destroying the tablets made by the finger of God. Previously, Moses had been on the mountain receiving the commandments of Yhwh while the people below were demanding a symbol (the golden calf) for themselves, a symbol that would make them like other people. This symbol is void of meaning except to be indicative of Israel's fetish for symbols.[14] This time Moses will return from the mountain with a small box that contains the two tablets of the law. It is a minimal symbol, a simple box, and it contains the words of the Decalogue written on two small tablets. Israel rejected the living voice of God and preferred symbolism to meaning. The Word of God is contained in a box, and God is reduced to a symbol.

The symbolism of the ark will continue to develop as Israel makes it larger and more aesthetically appealing.[15] David will build an elaborate cart for trans-

---

[13] Although the sign of circumcision was to be perpetual, the meaning can replace the sign. Deuteronomy 10:16 and Jeremiah 4:4, 9:25 contend for a circumcision of the heart as superior to the outward sign. In Romans 2:29, Paul will assert that embraced meaning is superior to the outward sign. Paul will assert that embracing meaning is spiritual, while embracing a sign or symbol is not spiritual. Romans 2:29 says, "Rather, a person is a Jew who is one inwardly, and real circumcision is a matter of the heart-- it is spiritual and not literal. Such a person receives praise not from others but from God."

[14] Israel is representative of humanity at large and in this case represents humanity's fetish for symbols. I refer to Aaron's response to Moses on why a golden calf: Exodus 32:24, "So I said to them, 'Whoever has gold, take it off'; so they gave it to me, and I threw it into the fire, and out came this calf!" There is no reason for the construction of the symbol; the need for the calf is an unnatural fetish for symbolic objects. This is instructive for us: idols have no meaning; they are vanity (hebel), as Qohelet would say. Kaufmann writes extensively on the Idol as fetish. Yehezkel Kaufmann, *The Religion of Israel from its beginnings to the Babylonian exile*, trans. Moshe Greenberg (New York: Shocken Books, 1960), 3-20.

[15] The human need for aesthetics must be governed by the ethical. Aesthetics are to serve human beings, but we enslave others for the sake of architecture,

porting the ark, which has become so large that it crushes a man when it falls from its cart.[16] The symbol of the ark is so powerful that it can boost the morale of an army, and yet so unpredictable that Israel loses its battle even when the ark is present (I Samuel 4). The ark is more important to Eli than the welfare of his sons and the continuance of his own life (I Samuel 4). In the grips of childbirth Eli's daughter-in-law views the loss of the ark as God's departure. She is a mixture of unnatural responses; she is giving birth to a son, but cannot rejoice because the ark is lost. In Hosea the glory of Israel is God's blessing of children (Hosea 9:11), and Eli's daughter-in-law prefers symbol (the ark) to new hope and life (her son).[17] David's co-opting of the ark is for the sake of his developing use of religion as a political asset amidst his ambitious efforts to build his empire. Jeremiah the prophet develops a theology that requires the complete dismantling and loss of all symbolism in order that Israel might come to know Yhwh. There is a text that suggests Jeremiah has either destroyed the ark, or knows that it has been destroyed (Jeremiah 3:16).

Metaphor and symbol both need revisiting so that the original meaning can be restored. To grasp meaning is spiritual and demonstrates spiritual intelligence. Meaning is always superior to the governing esthetics of symbols. A spiritual person is capable of living free of symbol, yet the use of symbol is unavoidable for the teaching of human beings and the formation of society. The Johannine community's non-sacramental practice of faith is spiritually superior to ritual and liturgical practices. Perhaps the oppressive forces around them contributed to their avoidance of symbol and spiritual practice.

---

landscaping, clothing, jewelry, treasures, and symbols of power. Symbols of a public nature promote culture and response. Paul Ricoeur, *Time and Narrative*, Vol. 1, trans. McLaughlin and Pellauer (Chicago: University of Chicago Press, 1984), 57-58.

[16] The falling of the ark is funny because it sits in contrast to the story of the falling statue of Dagon. The text never says God knocked Dagon over. I am suspicious of another cause. Are we to think that God can knock over Dagon, but not keep his ark on a cart? Perhaps God is not involved at all? Perhaps David's mighty men go in and knock over Dagon to build the people's awe of the ark as a symbol. David is a master propagandist, from his speech after killing Goliath to his speech after hearing Nathan's 'Davidic covenant.'

[17] The power of naming is displayed through Eli's daughter-in-law. An idolatrous people are hopeless without their symbols even in the face of life's ongoing hope found in their children; e.g., Eli's daughter- in-law.

Spirituality as Theological Practice

The claim to know God requires that the claimant display practices and behaviors that are reflective of spirituality. The first Adam was made a living soul, while Christ the last Adam was made a life-giving spirit (I Cor. 15:45). The archetypal Adam who fathered all humanity has been replaced by the archetypal 'son of man', the human being that imaged God within the confines of human finiteness, and modeled life and wholeness through a lived spirituality. We are now children of God. We are born from above and aliens to the practices of the world. (Romans 8:14, "For all who are led by the Spirit of God are children of God.")

Spirituality is dependent upon theological understanding and confirmed in practice. Christianity is meant to be lived and not just learned about. The attainment of theological understanding is accomplished through rigorous study of the scriptures. How do we do theology? From which perspective do we theologize? The answer to this set of questions is imperative for forming a base of theological understanding capable of producing spiritual practice. A theology that does not bring the life-giving spirit of God into the world produces an empty, powerless religion. The life-giving spirit of God comes into the world and changes humanity. Spirituality is viewable because human beings are changed and live according to spiritual practices that differentiate them from the rest of humanity.

The reading of scripture and the development of theological understanding is to be done with compassion or through the eyes of the powerless and oppressed of the world. Oppressed and powerless people experience reality void of the illusions of justice maintained by the powerful. The powerful too often maintain their power by oppressing others and living in a false reality that justifies their status and politics. Spirituality is not about easy answers. We are to seek solutions that are based upon carefully thought out theology that communicates the complexity of dealing with systemic problems in society.

Spiritual Authority

Through the prophet, the Spirit of prophecy speaks to the religious system from the outside. The prophet speaks as one without authority. This is so because the prophet is not part of the organized system or institution. The authority of the prophet is of heavenly (spiritual) origin and is not readily accepted or recognized by the institution. This is so because the prophet challenges the deification of the system. The Bible accepts the authority of the prophet as a legitimate expression of the LORD working in the world. The acceptance of the writings of the prophets into the canon of scripture attests to the need of the system for the word of the prophet.

As a prophet Jesus was questioned by the religious system of his day about his authority. Jesus' attack upon the buying and selling in the temple should be understood as a prophetic sign act in the tradition of the prophets. The act is performed by Jesus and speaks of a direct attack upon the temple system by God. Jesus then begins healing the blind and the lame. Upon his return to the temple he is questioned by the chief priests:

> And when he entered the temple, the chief priests and the elders of the people came up to him as he was teaching, and said, "By what authority are you doing these things, and who gave you this authority?" (Matthew 21: 23-24).

Jesus answered them, "I also will ask you a question; and if you tell me the answer, then I also will tell you by what authority I do these things." The manner of Jesus' answer is to redirect attention away from himself and back at his questioners. In their eyes Jesus is 'without authority;' he is not a part of the recognized religious system of his day.[18] His answer requires his questioners to state their opinion of a religious figure (John the Baptist) who is popular with the people, a religious figure who like Jesus stands outside the recognized religious institution of his day.

> The baptism of John, whence was it? From heaven or from men?" And they argued with one another, "If we say, 'From heaven,' he will say to us, 'Why then did you not believe him?' But if we say, 'From men,' we are afraid of the multitude; for all hold that John was a prophet." So they answered Jesus, "We do not know." And he said to them, "Neither will I tell you by what authority I do these things (Matthew 21:25-27)[19].

In a subtle manner Jesus has answered their question. The authority that worked in John the Baptist also works in Jesus. The authority of a prophet is the

---

[18] I use the term without authority and have drawn many of my concepts on the subject from the writings of Kierkegaard. The historical introduction to *Without Authority* expresses Kierkegaard's own views from various works. Soren Kierkegaard, *Without Authority*, trans. Howard and Edna Hong (Princeton: Princeton University Press, 1997), ix.

[19] It is notable that in this passage of scripture Jesus considers the spiritual authority of a prophet to be recognizable and to not require titles or association with any human constructed institution. Spiritual authority, then, is observable in the person that embodies the authority.

spiritual authority that Jesus possesses. At the same time Jesus exposes weakness in the religious leaders, which is that they feared people (the multitude), and they feared the prophetic Spirit that works outside the recognized religious system. Ultimately, their dependence upon the systemic guidelines for religious authority evidences their own failure to function as spiritual exemplars (leaders).[20]

God protests any religious system that limits God and his work with humanity to an identifiable system or framework because God is not servant to systems and conventions of human origin. Rather, the system is supposed to provide a vehicle for people to serve God, (not for people to rule over other people). Further, people can no more live by the rules of a designated system than they can live up to the demands of the law. The system is temporal; it is the failing reality of the now. The institution gives authority to its leaders; rather, the institution should recognize spiritual authority. An institution can serve well as long as it continues to recognize the authority that comes from God, who will work from outside the institution, yet in mercy will acknowledge the moral responsibility of the system. The crucial moment of decision for any institutional leader, or quorum, is to obey the living voice of the Spirit over the system's power to harm its own members.

The best of the prophetic tradition functions free of the institutionalized structures of religion. This said, the pursuit of a pure spirituality free from temporal powers cannot survive in an environment where authority of being is not recognized as superior to institutionally ordained leadership. The recognition of the constancy of tension in all systems, a tension that requires a choice to be spirit, permeates all of our existence in the now and not yet reality of a humanity in need of transformation.

The utopian demands of the spirit in a world where violence and death are suffered by the righteous are beyond the strength of a person who does not embody spiritual authority (maturity). The loss - or risking the loss of influence and power - at any moment for the moral justice that exhibits the reign of the kingdom is demanding; it requires self sacrifice and costly decision-making. The securing power of systems cannot make room for this kind of person; only a spiritual people are capable of living in harmony with spiritual authority embodied in exemplars.

---

[20] I have chosen to replace the overused, business-driven word 'leadership' with 'exemplar.' An exemplar lives the model for others to follow. This living model or image is contained in their person; it is an authority of being, a spiritual authority that does not require institutional acknowledgement or dependence.

Stories and the Spiritual Development of the G.O.D. International Community

First, I will contend that community births *ecclesia*.[21] The common practice of some churches to utilize power, money, and constraining declarative doctrinal statements to produce *ecclesia*, fails to generate a spiritually empowered community. The called out are people with a story based in the gracious acts of God in the past and the present. Their origin in the world does not find its beginnings in business practices and demographic studies, but in the story of the spirit found in the lives of the apostle, prophet, evangelist, pastor, teacher and laity. This spiritual dynamic lived out by people called to pursue the proclamation of the reign of God is a lived narrative for producing community. The distinctiveness of the community is attributable to the vision and call of the ongoing story produced as all pursue the work of God in their midst.

The revelation of God amidst the unfolding drama of human history is instructive for understanding the importance of human beings as participants in a story. The genealogies of the Bible are reminders of our participation in an ongoing family story, a human story. Stories are limited by the very medium which preserves them, whether that medium is, oral, written, or visual. The retelling of an event is always an artistic endeavor subject to the author's own limitations and purposes.

The complexity of history in all of its actuality cannot be completely recovered. Yet, the endeavor to uncover and learn from recorded history remains a necessary and valuable pursuit for several reasons. First, each generation is exposed to the relentless message of humanity's violence and can learn that, as human beings, we have not progressed. Second, our psychological need to uncover our identity (our story) through the immediate family lineage of parents and grandparents that preceded us belongs to the makeup of our being. The final need for uncovering history reveals to us the opportunity to make different choices than choices made by those that came before us. Choices will form our story, a story built upon the stories of others. Stories have a life of their own, and so they draw us in and cause us to participate.

Whether the story is written on paper or lived in the moment, we are captured by its power and become a part. This understanding should direct human beings to pursue a spirituality that is narrative-bound and beyond declarative statements. For Christians, that narrative is the stories of the Bible. The biblical stories speak

---

[21] I use the term *ecclesia* according to its original intent to acknowledge the 'called out ones', the moral learning community.

to us through the power of stories that help us to understand the story that is our own particular life.

Human beings as individuals and as part of humanity are participants in an unethical, immoral reality. The many sins that have entered the world have left us living in a world, a system, that has left us tainted; our hands are dirty, our innocence mingled with ambiguity. We are both victims and perpetrators of sin's power. Left before us are only difficult, life-altering, choices, many of which we are unprepared for and have not previously encountered. How then are we to live? Can we through Christ challenge the structures of sin's impact on every part of human existence and actually live the reign of God in a very broken world? I think so, if failure along the way can be included as part of our experience.

The development of character is essential for living a spiritual life. Yet, failure to live a spiritual life is always imminent, and, if you will, certain.[22] Focusing on character development is compatible with the teaching of scripture and fulfilled in the Spirit's work to conform us to the image of God in Christ. The abolition of sin begins with the establishment of character in human beings, a character that is consistent with the teachings and life of Jesus.

The development of a human being is initially the work of the mother and the father, or the primary caregivers, the immediate family (grandparents, aunts, and uncles), and (for some) the believing community. The various developmental elements that contribute to nurturing a human being towards wholeness are monumental in number and importance. Unfortunately, there is no certainty that any human being will make the right choices regardless of the dynamics of his or her upbringing. Nonetheless, the effort is essential because it is the responsibility of each generation to educate the next.

---

[22] The certainty of moral failure is, in my thinking, the result of social reality being corrupted by the entrance of many sins throughout human history, which marred the development of human beings captured in its power. Individually we have been created with the potential for doing good. However, as social, relational, and familial beings, our reality has been corrupted and causes us to seek truth from the perspective of darkness (to grope after God, as Paul states in Acts 17:26 (NRSV.) We are all victims of sin before we become perpetrators. Sin is not a genetic defect, but an inescapable and embedded power multiplied through the ages as humanity developed east of Eden. Sin in a sense is always a position before God, a negation of life, of the good. Sin is first inward, existential, a longing to be more than we are, a failure to live in harmony with God. Next, sin is outward and results in harm to others around us.

Spiritual Development and Character

The power of the Christian community to contribute to the character development of young people comes into play legally at the age of eighteen in our country. It is the time when Christian parents usually entrust the continued development of their children to a system of educators who are supposed to promote an accepted spirituality that contributes to the growth of Christianity as a part of the accepted social structure of the nation.

The narrative of these educational systems is linked to the narrative of the Christian community from which the young people came. The school where I taught did not represent a specific denomination and the student body represented over twenty various denominations. In effect, the power of displacement is more impacting as students must navigate new ground for their religious understanding.

A New Narrative and Character Development

A new narrative is essential for the ongoing development of the young people that attend The Institute for Global Outreach Developments International (G.O.D. International). The absorption of all other narrative traditions as possessing value is imperative to the ongoing effort to form young people around our particularly new narrative, which does not have a long history. My attempt was to expose the students to the best authors of each tradition without any prohibitive power from a denominational or religious identity. Nonetheless, my own influence was and is an ongoing power that directs the theological development of the students and community members.

As a community of believers who are primarily young and developing a new narrative for their religious community, they must learn the stories of the people whose lives were led in such a way as to produce the community. Having grown up in a denominational church and having served in several different denominations, I know that this was the intent of the early founders of most groups.

Stories of faith exhibited in courageous acts that were lived out in contradiction to the societal expectations of the nationalism found in the church allow the young people to reassess the impact of the 'world' upon their faith. These stories become part of the ongoing narrative produced by the burgeoning community of G.O.D. International. In order for spirituality to be derived from exemplars of faith, the stories told and preserved in the community must present a picture of an inner character that encourages others to act with courage in similar or relatable scenarios so that they might make the right choices.

The initial act of each community member to leave the security of an established tradition, the expectations of family, and enculturated societal behavior, enables students to sense or know that they are trying to form a new identity; yet their new identity is born out of a previous social construct. We carry 'our' history with us, learning to redeem and forgive makes our past 'an easy yoke.' It is likely that in time many will reconnect with the denominational practices with which they grew up, but for now they are exploring the potential for living differently. The difference brought on by the power of wealth and mobility, the exposure of young people to cultures across the globe, all play a role in the phenomenon of communities like G.O.D. International. It will be God's grace that carries them beyond the idealism that permeates youthfulness.

Character and Testing

Human beings when they arrive into the world are like 'blank white-boards'; they are people, and yet nothing of their life has been written on the board. They have some genetics, some hints of personality, some natural giftedness, and in relation to others will learn of their differences and limitations. The beauty of the white board metaphor is that it portrays the freedom of a person to engage in the process of accepting a story (their historical distinctiveness) while entering into history and possessing the power to write their own story as a connecting narrative. They must accept the family from which they came. They must accept the story of their origins as part of their story. They are also free to engage the world and write upon the blank slate of their own life. This engagement is the testing ground for character formation and spiritual development.

We know that God tested Abraham, the story of Job is reflective of life as a test, and the Bible records the testing of Jesus. These stories demonstrate that character is not fully formed until it is tested. This being so, then character is formed when the test is, if you will, passed. The failure to exhibit the kind of character that connects with God's holiness is to fail the test. I am writing on the premise that character development and spirituality are inextricably bound up with one another.

Character and Education

With this in mind, the essential element for contributing to the early character formation of young people is an education that is spiritually empowering, morally challenging, and socially constructive. It is an education that values human beings above all constructs of power. The education offered in the study of scripture with the guidance of a teacher is imperative for early character formation. The associative elements that contribute to character formation are the adaptation of a parent's narrative as part of the young person's narrative. This acceptance of identity bolsters the youth into an arena of early development that brings forth daily challenges to live up to the courageous elements of the parental narrative and avoid examples that are inconsistent with a life dedicated to serving God. The failure of Christianity in the process of forming young people is the neglect of the study of scripture as essential for human development. Our present educational system does not contribute to the development of critical thinking skills in relation to religious belief and practice. Bible students in denominational schools are indoctrinated into the denominational propositions and quickly educated in a particular discipline so that they might serve the aspirations of the denomination.

The importance of biblical education and of spiritual training for the ongoing mission of the church has been replaced with required religion courses that young people see as encultured structure and little more. Christian parents neglect biblical education and for the most part are biblically ignorant. The writing of a new narrative requires that the importance of biblical education precede the entrance of young people into the world as active participants in the formation of society. Further, it requires that biblical education be valued by a missional Christian community above 'secular' education. At G.O.D. International the concept is that four years to study the Bible prior to (or after) attaining other educational goals is a valuable practice.

Character and Academics

When attention is given by the family and the Christian community to character development over academic achievement, then education will have entered the spiritual realm of ethical practice. When Christian educational institutions withhold student graduation ceremonies from underdeveloped students and require these students to attend to character development and evidence a practiced spirituality prior to receiving a diploma that has already been earned academically, then our current education system will be moving towards a new narrative.

In western Christianity's educational systems students are tested for academic skills that promote competition and can earn reward apart from any proven character development. Life itself is a test and teachers cannot truly know their students if they do not live with them in a way that allows them to watch over their character development. I think that Jesus' method of 'Follow me' should be re-instituted into Christian education. Should an academic community be allowed to train Christian young people, if that community is not actively represented in the world fulfilling the great commission? Perhaps the only way we can achieve such an ideal is to incorporate the academic community and the church as a single entity. I mean a church where the academy is a permanent presence, a church where Bible school at an academic level is part of the church's facility and ministry. The separation of the church and the academy has invented the modern biblical scholar and his/her discipline. The loss to the church of her intellectuals has drained the church of her intelligence to be replaced with the magic of popular culture and blind positivity.

A Model for Developing a Spiritual Community

Spirituality runs concurrent with character development, testing, and time. Character development is experiential as a person responds to life's challenges. The tests of life that challenge us within the depths of our being are educational and require us to answer ethical challenges with both integrity and intelligence. The passing of time adds age and its benefits to the development of our spirituality. These three - experience, education, and age - establish some minimum standards for acknowledging spiritual authority.

Spirituality is not simply endowed upon a person as a complete work; rather, it is in the choices, the tests, and the unfolding of life where spiritual development occurs. Based upon this reasoning, experience, education, and age are all important when recognizing the spiritual authority of a human being.[23] Using the life of Jesus as a model for establishing a minimum age for spiritual authority is reasonable. The teaching and practices of the Rabbi's concerning the minimum age for authority is predominantly determined to be the age of thirty.

Experience is important for establishing authority and human experience is subject to the depth of a people's spiritual intelligence determined by the way he or she engages life. Spiritual intelligence functions in these three identifiable ways: developing an awareness of reality, feeling the burden of the brutality of humanity, and finally entering into that reality as people willing to be responsible for reality. To take hold of reality in all the fullness of a human being is to be carried by reality, by the spirit of God, by the unknown, by love's willingness to give, and to suffer so that the redemptive power of God might enter the world through suffering. In our community we call these the ABCs of spiritual intelligence (awareness, burden, and culpability).[24]

---

[23] The episode recorded by Luke about the boy Jesus is confirming of a forming spirituality. Although Jesus is impressive to the local religious authorities, his impression is limited to that of a curious twelve-year-old boy. Luke establishes the spiritual development of Jesus as concurrent with wisdom, years, and both divine and human favor. Luke 2:52, "And Jesus increased in wisdom and in years, and in divine and human favor."

[24] Intelligence as awareness, burden, and responsibility is set forth in numerous places within the writing of Ignacio Ellacuria as intelligent apprehension,

The concept of becoming 'historical people' is to acknowledge reality and to meet it with all that you are in an effort to bring the values of the reign of God into an erring reality, a false construction of existence, (in John's gospel) the world. People who live out their lives in the light of truth, and who face the false constructions of existence with resistance and truth will suffer positions of weakness and times of persecution. The biblical principle is that people who experience suffering undeservedly, and do so with an awareness of the power of truth, bring the redemptive power of God into the world. To be historical people is to subvert history, to change the direction of history, to write a new history, to tell a new story.

To be historical people is to follow Christ, become free of envy and self pity, and face life for the sake of others. A historical people accept their 'lot in life', according to Qohelet. In a sense, historical people live for those who come after them; they live for the next generation by living well in the moment with a heart for tomorrow.

Education in the scripture is essential for spiritual authority in a Christian community. This is so because we are people of the book. Theology is primarily done from the revelation of God contained within the Bible. I often tell my students that the Bible is only as good as the person reading it. This truth extends into the arena of character development and challenges purely scientific methods as superior for preparing the reader of the Bible.

Spiritual authority is essential for birthing and developing a community. Spiritual authority needs to be given to others and not held by a single individual. The eighteenth chapter of Exodus records the advice of Jethro to Moses and serves as an example for spiritual community development. The desire of Moses that all would be prophets is reflective of people not attempting to commandeer the voice of God for their own sake.[25]

When a person is called by God to participate in a community's ongoing story, the particularity of the community's calling needs to be accepted by the person. A community's vision is the impetus for a new story born of God's work

---

ethical stance and praxis. See, Kevin F. Burke and Robert Lassalle-Klein, eds. *Love that Produces Hope: The Thought of Ignacio Ellacuria,* (Collegeville, MN: Liturgical Press, 2006), 171-172. This same pattern is found in Kierkegaard's spheres of existence; the esthetic, ethical and religious. Stephen N. Dunning, *Dialectical Readings: Three Types of Interpretation,* (Pennsylvania: Pennsylvania State University Press, 1997) 15. I also utilized this pattern in my writings on global consciousness before I had read *Ellacuria* or connected my thoughts with Kierkegaard's spheres of existence.

[25] Paul rebukes the Corinthians for their failure to exercise a shared value system that enables even the least of them to make judgments concerning internal disputes within the community (1 Corinthians 6).

in humanity. Vision is not an ambitious business plan for success and numbers. Vision is essential for unity, and the limitations of our world require that God call people to particular tasks of service within a community setting. Vision is a spiritual grasping of the reign of God drawn into the now through community action and service. The calling of God does not allow for other choices; it is gripping, bound up in the life of the called.

In the attempt to be a spiritual community (Global Outreach Developments International), we value human beings and seek a world of justice and righteousness. For this reason, declarative statements of doctrinal conformity are less important to our community than the praxis of our faith. For example, I am thinking of those declarative statements that divide believers over questions about dispensationalist views on the timing of the coming of the Lord. Such seems unproductive, whereas attending to the needs of the suffering as an act of love done in the name of Christ is a sign of grace.

When confronted with male dominance, we practice a spirituality that interprets scripture from the view of women. We seek to liberate the voice of oppressed or dominated women and view this act as spirituality.

When confronted with poverty, we practice a spirituality that understands the condition of the poor as an injustice inflicted upon them by the powerful. This produces a reading of scripture always conscious of the temporal powers of human government.

When confronted with statistics that reveal the excessive practice of cesarean procedures, we practice a theology that connects with God's activity in the birthing process. We develop a ministry to serve women carrying children. We train midwives and doulas.

When confronted with global capitalism and its damaging effects upon entire nations, we practice a spirituality of awareness. We remember Jesus' and the prophets' approach to money as one of treating it as a dangerous power capable of derailing us from faith and spiritual practice.

When confronted with the power of symbols, we respond with a biblical understanding of symbols. Our theological conclusion is that the meaning behind the symbol is more important than the symbol, and it is to be stressed over the use of the symbol. Further, the complete dismantling of symbols is reflective of an informed spirituality that is aware of the misuse of symbols by the powerful.

When confronted with the incarceration of human beings, we respond with a theology developed from the Bible, rich with mercy, and informed of the injustices found in the prison systems of the world. We practice our response according to the view of Jesus. We visit and care for prisoners. We also note that Moses had an alternative to the penal institution with the cities of refuge.

When confronted with legally sanctioned injustice, we act according to the heart of an ethic drawn from scripture and our relationship with God our father. The current treatment of both legal and illegal immigrants is an example where breaking the law to defend the rights of the immigrant is a value for our community.[26]

Spiritual authority can only be recognized by others, that is, by those with an 'ear to hear' this is so because institutionalism limits and controls but cannot predict the moving of God. Spiritual communities can only be birthed through the ongoing revelation of God through his people. Spiritual communities have stories that are independent from social constructs of power. Spiritual communities do not need to be ruled by titled leaders or governed by professionals. Spiritual communities are formed around values that produce life within the daily affairs of living.

At present we have identified a number of values that we seek to live and teach. These are not meant to be comprehensive of our theological experience, but to be a work in progress. Briefly, these values are identified as: spiritual authority, conformation / becoming, one humanity, education, nonviolence and peace, community, narrative storytelling, liberation, united prayer and action, global consciousness, family, and self-sacrificial living. Our collective understanding of each of these values contributes to the contents of this work.

---

[26] Breaking the law is done in situations that require a human response to the presence of the alien rather than follow the nationalistic laws that are oppressive and harmful to the alien or immigrant. The disregarding of laws as an act of faith is subject to individual conscience and cannot be legislated as practice. To oppose the law is dangerous and costly to the offender.

CHAPTER 2
ACCEPTABLE WORSHIP

The title "Acceptable Worship" implies that not all worship practices are acceptable. I will present a theology that is representative of God's desire for all of his people to grow and mature in their spiritual journey and that demonstrates that learning to worship God is vital to spiritual growth. Although Christian worship has a variety of healthy expressions, care for the poor is the most important expression of Christian worship because love of God is expressed through love of neighbor. Further, I will present spiritual growth as accomplished when we learn to love one another through nonviolent living. To ignore the poor is an act of violence when a person has the power to relieve their suffering.

A basic educational pedagogy for my students at G.O.D. International is to challenge their conception of worship as being limited to singing and praying at Sunday morning church services. The importance of corporate worship is affirmed, while limiting worship to the sphere of Sunday morning practices is challenged.

Acceptable worship will begin with a brief study of Micah 6:6-8. In this part of my work I will present love of neighbor as an act of worship superior to religious ritual. This particular piece is one of the first pieces of scripture I require students to learn when they begin one of our school's programs. They are required to memorize the piece and to write a response to the lecture. The goal of the lecture is to move them from thinking worship is only accomplished within a corporate sacramental environment to accepting worship as an ongoing practice to be lived out amidst the movements of everyday life.

In the section on "Creativity and Nonviolence" I will discuss the move from ritual to maturity as a refusal of violence. This section will uncover violence at the root of human psychology and offer nonviolence as an alternative to the ideology of society which normalizes violence. In the next section titled "The Problem with Sacrifice," I will discuss the applicability of the theories of Rene Girard on mimetic rivalry, the scapegoat mechanism, and sacrifice. Sacrifice will be viewed as an anthropological phenomenon representative of communal violence acted out upon a single victim in order to relieve the tension of the presence of violence in all of its forms.

The final section of this chapter is a theology for the church's position in the world and the resulting effects when the church takes her proper place in the world. When the church takes its place alongside the poor, the church places itself between the two powers (the violent church and the state) that justify the use of violence. This is so because the poor exist on account of violence in both society and church.

Living Is Greater Than Ritual

The majority of people consider the worship of God to be a practice that takes place every Sunday in buildings around the world. We produce elaborate structures, services, and presentations in order to accomplish this task. The amount of monies and effort put forth for this endeavor is astronomical. I wonder what God thinks. Is he happy about all the 'sacrifice' put forth for this practice? I'm not sure God is entirely displeased, but I do believe we can do better and that in some instances God surely weeps at the enterprise of building church.

Micah 6:6-8 is a poetic text written to challenge our view on the value of rituals and focus us on the simplicity of worship.

> ⁶ "With what shall I come before the LORD, and bow myself before God on high? Shall I come before him with burnt offerings, with calves a year old? ⁷ Will the LORD be pleased with thousands of rams, with ten thousands of rivers of oil? Shall I give my firstborn for my transgression, the fruit of my body for the sin of my soul?" ⁸ He has told you, O mortal, what is good; and what does the LORD require of you but to do justice and to love kindness, and to walk humbly with your God?

This poetic piece can be divided into three major sections. The present verse listing of six, seven, and eight do well to make the distinction (in this case). In Hebrew poetry the parallel lines follow one another and can be synonymous, antithetical, or synthetical. Although these categories are not all encompassing of Hebrew poetic expression, they do serve as starting points for understanding.

It is not my purpose to instruct the reader on the varying practices for writing Hebrew poetry.

The first line is a question. An anonymous person (or Micah) asks what should be brought before Yhwh. The failure to qualify the 'what' as an offering or gift leaves the question open, so that the poem itself is to provide the answer. The next line intensifies the act of appearing before Yhwh as an act of submission. The person that comes before Yhwh does so in submission and with some unnamed thing. As the poem continues, the writer suggests possible gifts or offerings with which to appear before Yhwh. The suggestions are placed within the poem as questions that serve a rhetorical purpose. The reader must ask, "How do burnt offerings and calves benefit God?" The answer: "They do not." Like other prophetic pieces in the Old Testament, Micah views sacrifice as something other than appropriate for pleasing God.[27]

The next question poses the absurdity of abundance of rams or of rivers of oil as a way to please God. If we please God, we acquire his favor. So can God's favor be purchased through an abundance of rams and rivers of oil? If God were so arbitrary and capricious, then perhaps the ultimate sign of commitment would be to offer your own child? Micah has equated the idea that God's favor can be purchased through offerings as being equivalent to the detestable act of child sacrifice.

With a few poetic strokes written from his pen, Micah abolishes the practice of sacrifice and turns all ceremony into an act of deficiency.[28] Likewise he has

---

[27] The practice of sacrifice is viewed in the Old Testament as acquiescence on the part of God. God's acquiescence occurs because the people do not want to have an intimate relationship with Yhwh, but prefer to have Moses be their mediator. In Deuteronomy 5:29 Yhwh expresses himself with the most emotive phrase in the Hebrew language (literally 'who will give' usually translated as 'O that' or 'O that he would') and through use of this phrase indicates his desire that the people of God listen to his voice and obey, then sacrifice and law will not be necessary. God's first desire is that Israel becomes his people and he their God. This is expressed by the 'covenant formula' ('I will be their God and they shall be my people' or similar variations of the same thoughts). Jeremiah will assert that God's first desire and covenant did not include the practice of sacrifice. Jeremiah chapter seven is one such instance. Jeremiah 7:22-23: "For in the day that I brought your ancestors out of the land of Egypt, I did not speak to them or command them concerning burnt offerings and sacrifices. But this command I gave them, 'Obey my voice, and I will be your God, and you shall be my people; and walk only in the way that I command you, so that it may be well with you.'"

[28] The prophetic approach to sacrifice is that it is a product of human failure and not the desire of God.
Sacrificial practice is reduced to anthropological phenomenon in the biblical record. Jeremiah with others will propose that the sacrificial system established

mocked the idea that the giving of wealth enables a person to come before God or receive his favor. In the Bible wealth is not limited to money. Wealth in the Old Testament includes children, animals, and long life.

In verse eight Micah asserts that God has already told humanity what is good and what he requires. Although the knowledge of God comes via God's self-revelation, the knowledge of how human beings are to live is found implanted in our conscience and world. We are supposed to be intelligent enough to know that rituals are something that human beings practice when they either do not understand the world around them, or are signs to guide the young and uninitiated.

Micah teaches us that the favor of God is found in an ethical life that pursues a just relationship with the rest of humanity. This ethical life is lived out by practicing kindness and walking with humility before God. The three words used to direct us into this ethical life of relational connectedness with others are: justice, kindness, and humility. Justice is a relational idea and connects us to one another on the scale of equity. Kindness is an act that requires building relationship. Finally, to walk humbly with God is a relational concept and also implicitly requires walking humbly with humanity.

Micah's poem teaches us that God is concerned foremost with how we live in relationship to one another. A life that is lived properly gains God's favor and is superior to symbolic or ceremonial acts of religious expression. Micah's poem teaches us that God accepts an ethical life, grounded in relationship with humanity and God, as acceptable worship. Simply put, the institutional structures of religious belief and practice are annulled as the end goal of religious practice and human maturation.[29]

---

by Moses was not God's first desire but a result of the rejection of his reign in the human heart. See Jeremiah 11:3-5: "You shall say to them, Thus says the LORD, the God of Israel: Cursed be anyone who does not heed the words of this covenant, which I commanded your ancestors when I brought them out of the land of Egypt, from the iron-smelter, saying, Listen to my voice, and do all that I command you. So shall you be my people, and I will be your God, that I may perform the oath that I swore to your ancestors, to give them a land flowing with milk and honey, as at this day. Then I answered, 'So be it, LORD.'" See, Rene Girard, *Things Hidden Since the Foundation of the World*, trans. Stephen Bann and Michael Metteer (Palo Alto, CA: Stanford University Press, 1978), 30-47.

[29] Although this statement seems relatively strong, it is qualified by the words 'end goal.' The end goal of religious practice is not to be able to act as a priest in a religious setting or attend all religious meetings; the end goal is to live like a child of God at all times and in all places. Further, the end goal of all worship practices, including the institutional and ritual, are to move us towards an ethical life lived in harmony with God and man. Institutionalism and ritual serve as safeguards and tutors against the inevitable abuse of religious authority by the most well-intended persons. At the same time, institutionalism and ritual must

I (we) worship God when we love our neighbor as ourselves. We do this when we offer a sacrifice of 'self' and resist our insatiable desires for more and share the bounty of God's creation with one another. We do this when we lose the vanity of a self-identity that is found in externals and become whole in a world where so few know what it is like to truly be human. Micah is not alone in his anti-institutional stance on religious practice. Joining Micah are numerous prophetic statements found across the pages of the Old Testament.[30]

> For I desire steadfast love and not sacrifice, the knowledge of God, rather than burnt offerings (Hosea 6:6).
>
> [22] And Samuel said, "Has the LORD as great delight in burnt offerings and sacrifices, as in obeying the voice of the LORD? Surely, to obey is better than sacrifice, and to heed than the fat of rams (1 Samuel 15:22).

Worship is expressed as an ethical life lived out in the commands to love God and neighbor. Loving God is expressed through love of neighbor and enables us to fulfill our humanity, and the fulfillment of humanity is to image God.

Freed from the trappings of wealth, power, and the constraints of the 'world', people will begin to worship God by loving their neighbor. They will draw closer to understanding the idea that we are created in God's image. Created in God's image, we are the apex of his creative effort.

Human beings are more valuable than any idea, than any amount of wealth or power, and more important than any ritual practice. Only human beings carry with them the potential to be drawn into the being of God in Christ. God is invisible, but his image is carried about in human beings. You cannot love God if you do not love human beings. You cannot claim to worship God in purity when you cannot control your desires for more. The earth is the Lord's and all its fullness, and we are responsible for the distribution of its resources.

Recently I listened to a politician's attempts to identify with the working class people. She claimed to care for the needy people that she met and retold their stories to the public. The problem with this political leader was that she (with an

---

be constantly challenged by the demands of justice spoken by the prophets. Life is always lived out between two poles, one of necessity and the other of idealism. So, we pray 'thy kingdom come' as we live in the tension of a world not the way it is supposed to be.

[30] Anti-sacrificial passages include: Deuteronomy 5: 22; Deuteronomy 5: 28-33; Psalm 50: 7-15; Psalm 82: 1-8; Amos 5:21-27; Micah 6: 6-8; Hosea 2: 14 – 18; Hosea 6: 6; Jeremiah 6: 20; Jeremiah 7: 21-23; Jeremiah 11: 1-8; Isaiah 1: 9-17; Isaiah 43: 22-25; Matthew 9:13; Matthew 12:7.

income of 100 million dollars in seven years) already had the power to help the people she met but did not. Still, she desires more power, claiming she will help the masses. If she did not help when she already had more than any single human being could ever need, she will not truly be concerned for the health and welfare of the masses. In her defense, she is simply another politician in a long line of political rulers who have not known that God has chosen to govern the world through the royal law of love.

Creativity and Nonviolence: From Ritual to Maturity

The 'New Birth' is a creative act which is accomplished via the reciprocal initiative of God and humans. The reality of faith sewn into the fabric of creation and of every human being's staggering halt at the decision to faith is part of our psychological and spiritual makeup. It is at the point of decision, the 'yes' to God, when the dynamic or reciprocal engagement occurs.

Soren Kierkegaard offers some insight into the moral fabric of human beings and how we are to mature in Christ.

> Just as knowing oneself in one's own nothingness is the condition for knowing God, so knowing God is the condition for the sanctification of a human being by God's assistance and according to this intention. Wherever God is in truth, there he is always creating. He does not want a person to be spiritually soft and to bathe in the contemplation of his glory, but in becoming known by a person he wants to create in him a new human being.[31]

The first act of violence against God was also an act of violence against creation (even if self-inflicted by the first human beings). We can also say that any act of violence is an offense to the creator, an act against his good will and determination for human development.

I will argue that nonviolence is the 'principal component' for God's reign, whereas love is the second component and Spirit is the essential component. Some would want to place love as the principal component and the guiding ethic for people of faith. The problem with this thinking is that it does not consider that love is demonstrated and experienced via a growing relationship between two persons. Whereas nonviolence is an agreed upon principle and a mode of existence, and God has determined that human freedom be limited by God's

---

[31] Soren Kierkegaard, *Eighteen Upbuilding Discourses*, ed. and trans., by Howard and Edna Hong. (Princeton, NJ: Princeton University Press, 1990), 325.

benevolent desire for a world of peace. Nonviolence is a behavioral response that is imperative for life to flourish. Love cannot be practiced without nonviolence as both an accepted ideology and an acknowledged form of behavior that is preeminent for the reign of God. Love cannot be experienced unless violence is rejected.[32] I think this is one of the predominate messages of the Cross, if not *the* predominate message.

Prior to forming a relationship with God, the halt of decision places a person at the leap of faith. Faith is a relational connectedness to the one who is the object of faith. At this point relationship can begin. However, love has not yet manifested beyond the creator's initial culpability for creation; e.g., God must create an environment suitable for the created beings. In order for love to be practiced in a reciprocal manner, the creature must embrace nonviolence and recognize that to violate the gracious will of the creator is an act of violence.

When I claim that God's will is gracious, I mean that God does not always will every moment. Rather, God's will allows room for human decisions to participate in the unfolding of creation and existence. This wonderful freedom, which allows for us to image God by co-creating our ongoing existence with him, needs a guiding ethic (non-violence, love, and spirit).

God is like, and is, a good parent, one that allows his children to make decisions on their own. These decisions have a real and lasting impact on existence and for all of creation. Rather than dictate the lives of our children, we raise them to make decisions on their own. These decisions will have lasting impact and shape the direction a life will take. A good father and mother are happy to release their children to make their own decisions when they have reached the proper age and/or moment in life.

Until that time they are under the tutelage of their parents. Yet even the youngest children are aware of the freedom to violate the will of their parent. The potential for violence is found in the smallest toddler. The loving parent teaches the toddler non-violence before the child is aware of the reality of love. For example an eighteen-month-old child is taught not to hit other children long before the concept of love can be cognitively grasped or intuitively known. The fragility of the human body speaks to God's intentions for us to care for one another. Parents must teach nonviolence before they are able to communicate to their children the reality of love. The children are in the place where they might have some intuitive sense of love, but the concept itself cannot be communicated. If we cannot put a concept into words, then we do not understand the concept and have not learned it. Nonviolence is demanded by the parents, whereas love must be learned

---

[32] On the subject of God and violence I contend that God as a being is nonviolent. The violence we attribute to God is born of the cost imperative for creating free will beings and is part of the created order, but not inherent to the being of God.

and experienced. Nonviolence as a demanded behavior precedes our awareness of love. Likewise, nonviolence is demanded of us by our creator. Nonviolence is more than a concept; it is learned behavior. Jesus himself has become our teacher for this learned behavior that reflects wisdom acting with love.

The new birth and new creation metaphors of the Bible are synonymous terms in the sense that birth is a creative act, and every child born is a 'new creation'. The ongoing creation of human beings has been interrupted by their destructive will, or their 'no' to God, or if you will, their 'un-creation'. God wants to create in his humanity a people that do not practice violence. Creation, or the world we live in (if not the entire cosmos), is a reflection of human behavior. The moral behavior of Israel, throughout the Old Testament is consistently equated with the condition of the land. Violence is not a part of the world to come, nor is it a part of God's reign in the now.

Although love is considered to be the preeminent guide for Christian ethics, I contend that nonviolence precedes love as the preeminent ethic. This is so because of the tendency to identify love with justified violence in both church and society. Further, we as human beings must learn how to love, and the command to love our enemies removes any use of violence as a practice. Love suffers; God has suffered for our sakes, and violence refuses to suffer. Love is a choice and a willingness to identify the image of God in every human being. As human beings we love, experience being loved, and love because we learn to love. Love is a reciprocal relationship based upon acceptance of other persons for both their pleasing and unpleasing traits, whether physical, emotional, aesthetic, or intellectual. The relationship that experiences love is born of a choice to love. The bond of love created between a mother and child is fraught with pain and sacrifice on the mother's part. The child loves because the child is dependent upon the mother. The lesson derived from the mother-child relationship teaches us that love is born of suffering and dependence. Dependence can be a starting point for love because the dependent person experiences love in the world through the giving of the person on whom he/she needs.

Love is not just a mystical reality that enters our world. Love is a word descriptive of a person's willingness to suffer and give to another. God is love, because he is the complete embodiment of love's origins within existence. Jesus said that no one has greater love than to lay down his/her life for a friend. Love is measured in willingness to lose one's life on behalf of another. Again, love is sacrificial, and the recipient is dependent in some fashion upon the act of love.

I assert that love cannot be properly learned if nonviolence is not included as love's guiding principle. I will define violence as unrestrained force which harms the person that is on the receiving end of a violent act, whether an emotional, physical or ideological act. Restrained force with no intent to harm, and with care taken not to harm, can be accepted as a nonviolent act if force is used to preserve the life of the recipient of the act of force and if the restrained act of force is governed by love. It is not violent to wrestle drugs away from a person about to destroy him- or herself with the drugs. It is not violent to give a firm pat on the bottom to a child who does not want to listen to a parent (assuming the preceding qualifications are applied). As a practice, war always works with unrestrained force.

The Johannine community understood that love is taught. Their testimony is that they learned love from God and his acts of self-revelation as found particularly in Jesus, they wrote: "We love because he first loved us" (1 John 4:19). As a relational reality, love is dependent upon the source for its possibilities, who is God.

If our God is violent, then we will be violent. However, God has revealed himself to be opposed to violence. The Spirit of God that spoke through the prophets longed for a time when violence would be no more. The origin of evil runs hand in hand with the birth of violence.[33]

The first acts of violence according to the biblical mythopoeic stories of Genesis 1-11 must be read within their intended function, and not read literally for purposes of establishing history.[34] If this is understood, then the first act

---

[33] I think that within the limits of creation, God could not avoid the immediate failure of beings created in God's image. The loss of innocence (naivety) for limited, gendered beings, with a beginning is essential for human development. Once limitation enters the realm of existence, the possibility of failure is due to the finite limitations of created beings, particularly beings created in God's image. The relatedness to God given to human beings through the image of God enables humanity to form reality as they perceive it collectively. This being said, God chooses to create anyhow, and becomes culpable for God's erring creation. God is guilty of being merciful and granting us the choice to live. That choice requires our faith to see the one that is singularly complete and yet invisible to the created world in which God works. God's desire that we would have genuine or authentic relationship with God requires that we have authentic power to say yes or no to God. This power is essential for God's fulfillment of God's desires and brings the element of risk into the creation. God took the risk, and the human beings failed; now God is going to show God's self greater than our failure and redeem us. God will win us over through God's story found in Israel's history, Jesus the Christ, and the ongoing story of God's people.

[34] It is interesting to note that the peoples of the Ancient Near East were exactly like their gods. Their gods were male and female; they killed and used violence. The mythopoeic stories of Genesis depict a nonviolent God that creates people from the ground, and not from the blood of a dead god. My own opinion on the flood narrative is that it is a response to other flood narratives. The writer of these early narratives must respond to similar stories with a theology that represents the monotheism of Israel. It is written to present a God who places his bow in the sky to signify peace (to enter a man's tent and stand your bow upright meant

of violence was an act of human will against God as human beings sought self-autonomy, rather than trusting and learning from their creator. The second act of violence was one brother against another.[35] The flood narrative testifies to the human propensity for collective dominance that results in destruction if God does not intervene and destroy the evil or the violence. God's reason for the flood is because violence filled the earth. As the story of humanity unfolds, it is a story of violence, greed, power, dominance, hate, control over others to their hurt, the abuse of women and children, and the exploitation and destruction of the environment, which God created for humanity to live in. We might say that the Bible teaches us that the 'fall' was a fall to violence.

An Etiology for Ritual Sacrifice as an Anthropological Phenomenon

The Cain and Abel story is a study in the anthropological origins of sacrifice. It also reflects the book of Genesis' tendency to deconstruct misunderstood practices that were endured by God in his mercy, but are not God's desire for human beings. Genesis often serves as a counter-cultural text to the rest of the Bible. A simple example is Jesus' use of the early creation narrative to establish monogamy as God's first desire over the practices of polygamy and divorce.[36]

---

you did not come in peace). Likewise, the goal of the flood narrative is to teach that God will provide the seasons and chaos will not overcome us. The flood, then, is an anthropological fear based upon the large masses of water known as our oceans, and the unknown geology that reflects a time when the world's surface was underwater. The Bible is not interested in our geological questions. My personal opinion is that there was not a universal flood brought on by God for the intent of destroying humanity, nor does a small scale flood of a local region need be represented by the flood narrative.

[35] The failure of Adam and Eve is inward and existential, and it occurs prior to eating the fruit as Eve contemplates and reasons away the need to hear and obey. Adam's thoughts are not revealed to us; his actions confirm that he has his own reasons for disallowing God's instructions. Cain's failure is outward; the murder of his brother is an outward act that denotes the relational reality of all human action.

[36] The difference between remarriage and polygamy is that in Jewish society, a divorce allowed the man to be relinquished of responsibility for his former spouse; aside from this, men still took multiple wives; they just had them one at a time rather than all at once. Through the use of divorce men practice a form of polygamy that absolves them of their responsibility to the first wife. Thus, in ancient Israel to the early centuries A.D. the practice of divorce is more damaging than polygamy and less humane. The difference in modern societies is that women can live independently of men, so, divorce is not as damaging as polygamy.

The Cain and Abel story is representative of humanity's division. We are divided into two groups, the powerful and the powerless (simplistic but true). In the story, the 'possessor' kills the silent brother, who never speaks a word except via his blood.[37] Abel, whose life is like 'vanity' or 'worthless,' is taken by his brother in a jealous moment of rage (mimetic rivalry). Cain's rage is connected to his desire to practice religious ceremony his way, and not in the way that pleased God.

In the story, God had not asked for any form of sacrifice, yet Abel's sacrifice is approved by God. Two questions arise: Why do the first two brothers find a need to offer some form of sacrifice, and why does God *look upon* Abel's?[38] If we understand the early narratives to be etiologies for questions such as *Why have all cultures practiced sacrifice?*[39], then we can begin to approach the story in a way that leads to an interpretation that calls for sacrifice to be under scrutiny as an anthropological phenomenon. Couple this understanding with the fact that God did not request either Cain or Abel to bring a sacrifice, then the question becomes *Why did God approve of Abel's sacrifice over Cain's?*

It is also important to take note that the story includes the prohibition of eating the fat, which is found in Leviticus 7:25. Abel is approved because he did not eat the fat of the animals. On the other hand, Abel's sacrifice is in agreement with the Levitical regulations that require offerings of fat to be given to God when an animal is sacrificed. The tendency of the text of Genesis to deconstruct previous ideas is pertinent to our interpretation of the sacrificial act of Cain and Abel.[40] With these two points established, the Cain and Abel story can be interpreted through the lens of anthropology as an etiology for the phenomenon of sacrifice, and as a corrective for the sanctioning of sacrificial practice as the epitome of God's desire for worship.

At this point I will utilize the theories of Rene Girard concerning sacrifice as a scapegoating mechanism and a product of mimetic violence. Girard's theory

---

[37] The name Cain and the character of the murderous brother who bears the name is not coincidental; people that speak Hebrew would hear the sound of the name and understand his name to speak of his character. Cain is a possessor, someone interested in acquiring more. Abel is 'worthless;' his life and voice are reduced to nothing but an act of oppressive violence that begins with anger and culminates in murder. Abel is a scapegoat for Cain's uncontrollable need for violence, because he will not utilize the pressure relief valve of ritual sacrifice.

[38] In the Hebrew text God simply *looks upon* Abel's sacrifice, while *he does not look upon* Cain's.

[39] Accepted etiologies in the early text of Genesis include answers as to why snakes crawl on their bellies and women experience pain in childbirth. In the Cain and Abel story we find an etiology for violence.

[40] My opinion on Genesis 1-11 is that these proto-historical narratives are written during the exile in Babylon.

begins with the observation that human beings are mimetic creatures. We are not instinctual creatures, but insightful creatures that need to be taught. As mimetic creatures we need a model to follow or copy. If the model is greater than us, then we seek to destroy the model so that we will not have to face ourselves in our failure or take on the challenge of living up to the model. Cain, the older brother, does not want to learn from his younger brother. Likewise, older civilizations do not want to learn from the younger and smaller Israel.

This is particularly interesting in the Cain and Abel story because the story inverts the preeminence of elder and younger.[41] Abel as the younger brother sets a model for the older brother to follow, because God looked upon his offering, but he did not look upon Cain's.[42] Although God did not ask for the offering, he 'looked' upon Abel's. The story continues to unfold and God speaks kindly, lovingly, and fatherly to Cain. Cain, however, will not receive God's instruction and commits the first act of violence from one human being to another.

At this point the text is surely pointing to the law as a place for receiving instruction, even though the law, like Abel's sacrifice, is a product of human need and not solely the expressed desire of God for humanity. Law and sacrifice, then, belong to the arena of human need, a need which God looks upon, while seeking for us to grow beyond. God's words to Cain are to be considered:

> [5] but for Cain and his offering he had no regard. So Cain was very angry, and his countenance fell. [6] The LORD said to Cain, "Why are you angry, and why has your countenance fallen? [7] If you do well, will you not be accepted? And if you do not do well, sin is lurking at the door; its desire is for you, but you must master it" Genesis 4:5-7.

Based upon arguments to this point, I suggest that Cain is to understand that doing well is pleasing God, even if it means learning from his younger brother, and even if it means practicing in a ritual for which he does not understand the significance. We are our brother's keeper, or we will become his/her murderer. Religious ritual has its place, but only as a teacher to point to greater truths.

Cain has begun a cycle of violence that God wants to interrupt with forgiveness. So, God puts a mark of love and forgiveness on the first murderer so that no one will harm him. God desires to teach Cain through love and forgiveness. Abel's blood has cried out from the ground, and God has heard the voice that

---

[41] This is a regular practice in Genesis to invert the law of the firstborn; e.g., Jacob and Esau, Ephraim and Manasseh.

[42] I am basing the 'look' upon the Hebrew text and avoiding the word 'regard.' The Hebrew text reads that God looked upon Abel's sacrifice but not upon Cain's.

never spoke throughout the text. In this way, Abel represents the silent voices of all those who suffer under the hand of violence. In the text, Abel has died for his brother's forgiveness.

Violence is an escalatory cyclic phenomenon in our world. Once blood is shed, violence begins to escalate. Violence cannot do anything but escalate. Violence is halted when it becomes so horrific that human beings cease to participate in its continuance.[43] For example, the United States would not halt its activities to end the aggression of the Japanese until the violence of the atomic bombs was released.

Hitler seems to have understood something about the power of violence, and made entire people groups into scapegoats and into sacrificial offerings to the god of violence. Only when the rest of humanity became horrified by his actions or were attacked did they act to stop him. I am of the opinion that the church in Germany failed because it did not challenge the anti-Semitic rhetoric and oppression of Hitler's regime with immediate refusal to cooperate. Nonviolence is not cowardice, but a demonstration of power that trusts in resurrection without fear. Martyrdom is an act of faith, not self-hatred; it is the exception and not to become a normalized goal for Christian life or development.

With these things in mind, then we can see how sacrifice functions as a temporary halt to the escalating violence released through the power of sin. A scapegoat is chosen, and in an act of ritual violence the life of the scapegoat is taken. The ritual gives a sense of sacredness to the mundane act of slaughtering an animal.[44] This sense of sacredness achieved through sacrifice allows human beings to find relief from the violence of sin, even to forgive the guilty party.

Violence can be halted temporarily by ritual sacrifice, or it can escalate to a place where the horrific end arrives. However, it is only temporary because

---

[43] The book of Judges and the story of the silent concubine draw out this truth. The violent abuse of a woman escalates to the point of near genocide upon the Benjamites. Only when Israel sees the horror of their violence do they stop. However, the violence against women continues as unsuspecting girls are given to the remaining Benjamites in a kind of approved kidnapping. See Judges 19-21. I think the story of Samuel hacking Agag into pieces (1 Samuel 15) reflects Samuel's understanding of the need for a horrific act to halt violence (thus, the use of *herem*, the complete destruction of everything), and the removal of profit from Saul's warring activities.

[44] The act of killing animals can become a mundane practice when repeated on a daily basis; however, the use of ritual refuses to allow killing of animals to become mundane. I once had one of my mission students slaughter a pig for a feast. He had never killed an animal before. The experience for him was not mundane, but awakened him to the utter brutality of violence when life is taken. The ritual of animal sacrifice also draws a distinct line between the value of human beings over the value of animals. Animal life can be taken to support the 'shalom' of human life.

violence is cyclic. Neither the scapegoat nor ritual sacrifice is sufficient to bring a complete end to violence; even the horror that brings the halt is temporary. Jesus' way of nonviolent resistance, of absorbing the violence into oneself, is capable of halting ritual sacrifice. This can be seen as a turning point in history, as ritual sacrifice has faded from human practice except in very remote primitive peoples. Jesus' act of absorbing the violence into himself and bringing forgiveness to all who believe is also capable of ending violence for those who will learn that violence is an intolerably abhorrent practice that in no way is a reflection of God's image. However, becoming the scapegoat, being righteous like Abel, following Jesus, and picking up our cross as a way of living to be modeled will eventually, with God's help, bring an end to violence

Called Alongside:
The Church's Position in the World

Torah, Prophets, the Writings, and Jesus have very little to say without the inclusion of the poor. This alone should awaken our attention to the preeminence of the poor in the practice of theology. Jesus reveals to all of us the potential in each of us to exhibit what it means to be human. Jesus is the full expression of humanity in his life and teachings. I am fond of saying that, "Jesus was a really great human being."[45] The incarnation is both the coming of God into the world and the fulfillment of humanness. Jesus is our model for living within the context of a human life with all its varied particularities. He experiences being human without exception, yet his origin is 'from God' and his essence is God.

When God enters the world to walk among us, he positions himself alongside the poor. Like the prophets before him, social justice is a matter of urgency and not merely a utopian dream. Jesus and the Torah direct our faith towards God as an object of love, and then our love for God is displayed via a faith that is centered on the liberation of all human beings, particularly the poor. The prophet Micah presents acceptable worship as relational acts among human beings where doing justice and loving kindness produces a walk before God that is bereft of all pride in self. In three verses Micah has abolished any form of sacramental worship as necessary for proper living before God (Micah 6: 6-8).

---

[45] This phrase seems to be passed around and accredited to a number of liberation theologians like Ignacio Ellacuria, Dom Helder and Osacar Romero. I began making the statement prior to reading any of these gentlemen. In a world of limited words where people study and have thoughts, it is inevitable that people will develop similar statements.

In Genesis, God stops short of ending the lives of Adam and Eve by 900 plus years. God holds off on the immediacy of death's final blow because he desires to walk with them and teach them how to live so that they can be redeemed. Their poverty of spirit leaves them with a murdered son and a murdering son. The mythic nature of the story divides humanity into two distinct groups: those whose lives are of no value and those who wish to dominate the earth via the city and violence. Before God speaks to Cain the murderer, he (God) hears the voice of innocent blood crying from the ground. The loss of Abel has reached the heart of God, but God also loves Cain and forgives the first murderer.

The poor of the world are the oppressed victims of global wars, global economics, and political powers reigning from cities around the world. They are humanity's Abels. In Exodus where God's self-revelation is the underlying concern for God's behavior, God hears the cries of slaves suffering under the empire building of an earthly king.

In the prophets, the nation, which God knew like no other, has failed to be the people of God, and they have developed a dominating system of social stratification that divides humanity into the powerful and the powerless (the violent and the victim). In the book of Amos, the poor are left destitute, while the rich prosper in silver and will not even provide shoes for the feet of the poor (Amos 2:6). In the book of Jeremiah, the rich are guilty of setting traps to ensnare human beings by taking away their right to the goods of the land (Jeremiah 5: 26-28).

When Jesus begins his ministry in Luke 4, it is with the words of Isaiah (chapter 61) that Jesus proclaims 'good news,' which is based upon the Torah's teaching concerning the complete alleviation of debt. The acceptable year of the Lord is a reference to the practice of Jubilee. If we understand that the teaching of the law and of Jesus is pedagogy for something far greater, then the law or teaching is only a starting point from which to begin practicing justice. It is the hope pieces of the prophets that envision the utopian reality of the reign of God. The Torah, and Jesus' teaching are not the end result; they are the path to the end, which is the reign of God in every human heart.

The Torah and the life and teachings of Jesus are both corrective efforts to establish the reign of God. When we understand this truth, then we can see that the reign of God is accomplished when the present systems of this world are abandoned for a life of nonviolence and faith. God's plan for human beings to be nonviolent creatures is fulfilled in God's own self-revelation delivered in the story of Jesus' life, death and resurrection. This revelation is not just a lesson for human behavior; it is the intimate communication of God's being immersed in, but separate from, the created order.

A Nonviolent God

The utopian vision of the prophets (e.g., Isaiah 2:4) is only possible if God is non-violent. We are capable of nonviolence only if God is nonviolent. This is so because we are created in his image and the best we can do is live according to his image. Once we understand our own responsibility for creation as creatures, then we can grasp the concept of God as nonviolent, kind, and benevolent.

The concept of nonviolence and a nonviolent God is the principle component to the reign of God. The reign of God cannot exist with any type of violence; it can only tolerate violence for the sake of redemptive activity. The toleration of violence must come to an end before God's reign is fully established. The essential component for the reign of God is 'spirit.' To be spiritual is to image God in the world, so that others will see God in you. At this point it is important to remember that God came into the world and was not recognized because of his position alongside the poor and oppressed. He was not recognized because he proposed an ideology for living that the world would not accept. Jesus' concept of the reign of God was so radical that the religious authorities condemned him for blasphemy, and the political powers considered him a threat to the Pax Romana.

Although the prophets portray utopia, Jesus' teaching was not so idealistic as to be unachievable. Utopia is on the other side of our willingness to follow Jesus in the now. Some fear such a challenge as a 'Kingdom Now' teaching. The problem is that fearing the presence of practicing the reign of God in the now is to reject the reign of God. I am not saying humanity is solely responsible to establish the reign of God; I am saying that we should do as much as we can to live according to the teachings of the scriptures and Jesus. This is our calling; it is our vocation; it is being a Christian. Who can say how much good might come of the willingness of some or many to actually live out the teachings of God revealed in Christ.

In Harm's Way

When the 'church' takes its place alongside the poor, then it has put itself in harm's way. The church that lives alongside the poor will find itself with two opponents. The first opponent is the church that justifies the use of violence and accepts violence as an unalterable reality for the present age. The second opponent is the political powers of government and economic powers like corporations.

The church that takes its position alongside the poor is now placed between the poor and the powerful. The powerful include the church that accepts the use of violence. This is an interesting distinction within the church and is worthy of some analysis.

God desires to rule by winning human beings over to him, by having them submit to his spirit willingly. In contrast, people rule over people with unjust systems that are supported by violence. The church that supports or actively argues for the justification of violence is on the side of the temporary powers of the political systems of the world. I am speaking in particular of the church that practices 'state theology' and grants to the state religious legitimacy. This is a complicated issue as is reflected in the theology behind the Kairos document of South African church leaders.[46] The difference between a nonviolent person and a violent person is that one will kill intentionally and the other will not. One is behaving as child of the murderer Cain, and the other is a victim like Abel, the righteous.

The poor are not active participants in organized violence. Rather, the poor are victims of violence. The wealthy and powerful justify the use of violence to maintain the order that keeps them wealthy and powerful. The poor do not practice organized violence. One exception is when poor young people, mostly men, are indoctrinated with an ideology and given a gun.[47] The ideology can be democracy, communism, socialism, a dictator, an aristocracy, or a monarchy. The poor youth desire a better life, and if some wealthy politician or aristocrat had not indoctrinated them with an ideology that promised justice and armed them with weapons, they probably would not have participated in organized violence.

The violent church does not want to take up the vocation of God and live alongside the poor. The presence of violence, particularly the acceptance of violence as justifiable, is indicative of the absence of love. God is first introduced in Exodus as a God of slaves. They are his people, and he longs to be their God. The violent church establishes a kingdom of this world and enforces its rule with acts of violence. The violent church aligns itself with political powers (like Assyria). The violent church trusts in the strength of their nation's military to ensure peace (horses or the modern equivalent of tanks). The violent church prides itself on the work of its hands (self-sufficiency based upon economic wealth). The violent church is orphaned and without God in the world (except for mercy). Hosea records this trilogy of idolatry and violence in his final hope piece.

> 2 Take words with you and return to the LORD; say to him,
> "Take away all guilt; accept that which is good, and we will offer

---

[46] R. Scott Appleby, *The Ambivalence of the Sacred* (Oxford: Rowman and Littlefield, 2000), 37-40.

[47] Another possible exception is rioting; however, rioting is an activity of social groups that do not necessarily suffer abject poverty.

the fruit of our lips. ³ Assyria shall not save us; we will not ride upon horses; we will say no more, 'Our God,' to the work of our hands. In you the orphan finds mercy." (Hosea 14: 2-3)

The masses of people in the violent church are formatively immature in their expression of Christ in the world. The masses of people in the violent church are usually intellectually bound by mythical/literal interpretive methods, and are unwilling to lose their lives in order that they might gain life. The poor will let their children suffer and die when they cannot obtain medicine worth two dollars, whereas the powerful would commit crimes and acts of violence in order to obtain the two dollars. The mindset of the poor is aware of the cyclic power of violence practiced by the powerful. They know that only when the retaliation of the powerful against the poor becomes horrific will the violence cease. They also know that the halting of violence by the powerful is only temporary. So, they do not practice violence to obtain their needs because they know that the violence they would ignite in the powerful will pale in comparison to their present suffering.[48]

Often the poor accept their poverty as their lot in life and do not attempt to overcome it. The reason for this is found in the oppressive nature of poverty. Poverty kills the spirit of hope, and lack of education renders intellectual challenges by the poor to silent suffering. The task of the church in positioning itself alongside the poor is to give them the voice that they have lost amidst their suffering. We are to articulate that which is lost to their silence.

If the church does not see the poor as the lost treasure for which a man sells all that he has to purchase the field which contains it, it does not understand the value God places on human beings. We human beings are the apex of creation, God's crowning achievement. The irreplaceable uniqueness of every individual human being is a reflection of God and his creative power. The inestimable value of every human being is weighed against the sacrifice of God himself upon a barbaric instrument of torturous death. We must not be caught selling humans for a closet full of clothes, a jewelry box full of gold, an overpriced luxury car, or a summer home. The person who images God loves people, all people. The person who loves God loves those who are caught in sin that is often a product of society's injustices.

---

[48] The poor in third world nations often receive threats that their homes are on property owned by others and that they are subject to immediate eviction and bulldozing. The poor are already the victim of socio-economic violence and would prefer to avoid combative violence. They know the powerful do not value their lives. They know the powerful will use violence to maintain the system that insures their wealth.

The second opponent of the church is the political powers of the state. The political powers of the state will rise up against the church that positions itself alongside the poor. This is so when the nonviolent church begins to bring the liberation to the poor, something that the state in all of its brazen power could not. When the church demonstrates a manner of life for the governing of people that surpasses the state's power, the church will find itself suffering the wrath of the state. The church is recognized as a revolutionary power because it liberates the voice of the poor to be heard in the public arena. When the poor learn to articulate their suffering, the violent powers of the world cannot bear the guilt and seek to silence their voice.

Conclusion

We Christians all acknowledge Jesus as King. Unfortunately most forget that our king wore a crown of thorns. It is only as we learn to worship God through living in relationship with the poor that the church will lift itself from the world and function as a witness to the presence of the reign of God. Living alongside the poor allows the church to mature and leave behind the scapegoat practices of basic symbolic instruction. Basic symbolic instruction belongs to those newly initiated into the faith.

This being so, some of the ritual practice of the church is useful for basic instruction when first working with the poor. However, the legitimacy of ritual must not become a way to control the masses, but only a tool, a starting point to bring them into a way of living that is pleasing to God. We are admonished by Paul to present our bodies as living sacrifices. This type of spiritual worship culminates in becoming living examples of Christ for others to follow. Our lives belong to God as living epistles and our bodies as walking temples where God dwells. Human beings are mobile, like the tabernacle in the wilderness. God reveals himself through human beings. His completed revelation is found in his own humanness through Jesus Christ.

Like Jesus, we are to find ourselves positioned before God and in harm's way, as we conquer the instinctual nature of the 'flesh' to become spiritual people whose very lives are an act of worship. Because we find God's servants placed between the powerful and powerless, crying out for love and justice, we like Jesus cannot respond in any other way to the impending violence than to act in nonviolent ways. Our nonviolence is not passive, but assertive as we insist upon the right of the poor to live and to be heard and to share in the bounty of God's earth. The reign of God is a reign of justice and righteousness, and worship is reflective of the pursuit of this activity. Amos says this well and renounces sacrifice and Israel's ritual religious practices. He says:

> [24] But let justice roll down like waters, and righteousness like an ever-flowing stream. [25] Did you bring to me sacrifices and offerings the forty years in the wilderness, O house of Israel? [26] You shall take up Sakkuth your king, and Kaiwan your star-god, your images, which you made for yourselves; [27] therefore I will take you into exile beyond Damascus, says the LORD, whose name is the God of hosts (Amos 5:24-27).

CHAPTER 3
THE ART OF SUBVERSIVE NARRATIVE STORYTELLING

In the process of educating the students at G.O.D. International we expose them to interpretive readings that view the biblical narrative as a subversive document. Prior to the articulated development of a hermeneutical method, the students are exposed to the concept of reading the Bible as literature, followed by interpretive readings that expose the subversive nature of the narratives. The following chapter is an offering of those types of readings.

I have often said that storytellers rule the world. This statement requires some explanation for it is certain that men have ruled the world through violence and not through the communicative device of storytelling. While this is so, the power of stories is exhibited by the way the powerful have utilized them in order to establish rule over human beings. The myth of the hero is often the first aspect of storytelling that facilitates the rise to power of a leader. The myth of 'destiny' connected to the ruler's birth and childhood also contribute to the story. Throughout history those who have ruled with force and power have cultivated myth to affirm their separateness from other human beings.

Through the art of subversive narrative storytelling the dominant voice of history is challenged by an undercurrent of another story. The subversive narrative story is the expressed voice of opinions and thoughts that the 'powers' would not allow to rise to prominence, were they aware of their actual meaning. Although storytelling can be equated with a fanciful imagination, the art of subversive narrative storytelling challenges the socio-economic, religious, and political powers. Further, such stories often tell the story of those whom history ignores, such as the poor, women, the conquered, and the ethnically different.

I will begin this effort with a semi-philosophical piece on the function of subversive story telling in relation to the myths of redemptive violence and progress. This section is a basic epistemology for my understanding on the role of subversive storytelling.

The Bible is such a document and contains many stories that fulfill the qualification of being artistically constructed, intentionally subversive narrated stories. In the following pages I will explore a number of such stories as subversive narrative art. One of my favorites is the commonly referenced example of Solomon's wisdom from 1 Kings 3.

The rise of the new movement to later be called Christianity also required some artfully constructed subversive storytelling in narrative form in order to simultaneously record an approved version and a subversive version of the events that caused the deaths of Ananias and Sapphira. The approved element of the story satisfies the ears of the powerful, while the subversive version undercuts the assumed reading of the story made by the powerful. The educated awareness or the social perspective of the hearer makes the difference for how the story is received.

The entire books of 1 and 2 Samuel are replete with subversive stories, of which two will be explored in the following pages. The first story is from 2 Samuel 2:11-17 and will explore the absurdity of the relationship between living warriors and dead heroes. The second is from 2 Samuel 5:22-25. This story reveals the commandeering of the voice of God accomplished by the state and its leaders.

These stories are explored under section headings appropriate to the stories purposes as subversive art. The first section is an effort to help the reader engage stories as subversive art through the tool of literary analysis. I will utilize the stories of Solomon's wisdom and the deaths of Ananias and Sapphira for this section. The second section is an effort to help the reader question historical claims based upon the manner in which history is told, which is from the point of view of the powerful. I will use the myth of dead heroes from 2 Samuel 2:11-17.

The third section is the spiritual quest to locate God in history. Because God has revealed himself in history and the Bible records this story, it is imperative that people know how to find God amidst a history recorded by the powerful. The last story I will explore is the encounter between God and Pharaoh. I will submit that within the unfolding encounter God is not found in the acts of power, but in the acts of mercy. During the presentation of these ideas I will argue that only a compassionate reading is able to uncover the subversive nature of a story. I will conclude with a summary on reading the Bible as a record of subversive storytelling.

The Function of Subversive Storytelling

The art of subversive narrative storytelling is the essential element for valuing understanding above knowing and cherishing ongoing communication over the totalitarian power often used by political and religious institutions over their subservient members.[49] Political and religious institutions are, in part, the outgrowth of the failure of humanity to maintain an ongoing story that continually combats myths of redemptive violence and myths of progress.[50] At the same time, the institution is an attempt to maintain the cultural values and language of the previous generation's experience through the violence of finality by defining the limits of knowledge.[51] At this point the new generation no longer experiences life in the same fashion as the previous generation. Rather, they are subject to the limits placed on them via the teachings and dogmas.

The teachings and dogmas of the past are seldom legitimate universal concepts, and if they are universal concepts, the limitations placed on them for the sake of cultural control are damaging to the continued growth of the people. Usually the limiting aspects of institutional power are maintained through the enforcement of adherence to written statements. These statements can become canonized objects accorded divine power. Examples include the U.S. Constitution and the statements of faith of religious sects or denominations.

A subversive narrative story brings lived experience in some form to the collective elements that contribute to knowing. Contributing elements to knowing are: guiding cultural and political myths, limits on terms or words for communication (dominant language), ethnocentrism, sectarianism, and educational systems that serve the collective politic and not understanding. Because the few dominate the many through the collective elements of knowing that perpetuate the myths of redemptive violence and progress, the subversive story is the unexpected power

---

[49] I am using the word 'knowing' to refer to objective knowledge and the word 'understanding' to refer to more subjectively integrated reflection on life's questions.

[50] Walter Wink, *Engaging the Powers* (Minneapolis: Augsburg Fortress Press, 1992), 13-32. The myth of redemptive violence is a termed used by Walter Wink to express the ideology that violence is an unavoidable necessity for existence. Jacques Ellul, *Reason for Being* (Grand Rapids: Eerdmans, 1990), 60-69. The myth of progress is the idea that humanity is actually progressing as beings, that our species is developing better human beings.

[51] The need for institutions will be unavoidable until the world is transformed at the end of the present age when Christ appears. The problem is to assume that the institution as a form of government can rule in an ever-changing human experience without being continually revised. Established longevity for an institution can be a sign of stagnancy as much as it can be a sign of success.

that challenges the status quo by communicating a real experience that represents the human voice amidst the power of institutions and governments.

In order for a story to be subversive, it must first appear as simple and contain elements that reflect the dominant culture's values and language. It is the redefining of language through the artistic communication of the story that becomes the ultimate subversion. To redefine language is to control the manner in which thoughts are constructed via language. For this reason, a subversive story can be heard on two levels. First, the dominant culture hears the story and does not immediately detect its subversive nature. Second, the common people hear the story and their understanding interprets the story as confirming their experience and challenging the claims of the dominate culture. Subversive narrative storytelling is an art utilized by those persons who have forsaken the myths of redemptive progress and violence, and who have identified the human element to be most alive in those persons whose voices have been silenced through the cultural politic.

Reading Biblical Stories as Subversive Art

1 Kings 3:16-28 - A Story Of Wisdom?

In order for a story to be subversive it must first appear as simple and contain elements that reflect the dominant culture's values and language. It is the redefining of language through the artistic communication of the story that becomes the ultimate subversion. For instance, in 1 Kings 3, when the poor hear the word 'prostitute,' it means 'oppressed woman.' The word 'king' means a person mad with power, and if the uneducated were educated, then they would use a word for king like 'demagogue' or 'megalomaniac.' The execution of justice in the ears of the oppressed is not justice served, but injustice inflicted upon the powerless. The death of the one oppressed woman's son is a criminal tragedy for which Solomon's governing is responsible, yet the tragedy of the child's death is ignored by Solomon. In this case language is silenced by the powerful that regard the life of some as but refuse. The myth of redemptive violence is made plain through the silence on the cause of one child's death and the sword bearing solution to take the life of the living child offered by Solomon to settle the dispute between the two women. In the case of the New Revised Standard Version (NRSV) reading of this story, the word 'awe' is not inspirational nor is it admiration; rather, for the powerless, it is fear.

Some basic literary analysis will be used to explore the subversive nature of the story from 1 Kings 3:16-28, which is traditionally provided as an example of Solomon's wisdom. The story is subject to two readings; the first is a legal reading, and the second is a compassionate reading. A legal reading begins with two women who have a conflict and bring their case before the king. The king is now a judge and is hearing a case and receiving testimony. The first woman to speak informs the king/judge that there were no witnesses. She recounts a tragedy (the death of a child). She makes a claim that a crime was committed (her child has been taken), and she is a victim. The women begin to argue before the king and are portrayed as emotionally unreliable. The king passes a summary judgment that reveals his supreme power over life and death. The story ends depicting the wisdom of the king and proclaiming that God was with him.

A compassionate reading begins with a picture of two oppressed women without husbands, impregnated by men who have no concern for their offspring or for the health of society. The women must stand before a king who is seated and surrounded by the trappings of power. Under his rule these women suffer abuse, and in their life they are barren of a proper male relationship. A compassionate reading hears the voices of the two women. The first is a submissive voice; her speech begins with a tone of respect to the powerful king. Further, she demonstrates through her recounting of the events clarity of mind, and the attentive reader can hear certain words and explanations differently than the legal reading.

The first woman to speak will say that the other woman lay on her child. The children are positioned in her story at the breast of each woman (verse 20). Further, she awoke to 'nurse' her child, while the other woman is said to have lain on the child. Two mothers are alone, no men present; the women's bodies used for a fee so that they might survive under the rule of the great king. How did the child die? Was the one woman psychotic in her pain and guilty of killing the child? Did she accidentally lose her son as she lay nursing him in a state of despair and exhaustion?

Neither of the women is allotted a name. They are but nameless characters in the presence of the king. When this story is approached as a carefully crafted work of subversive narrative art, then the development of the women's characters offers the reader enough information to discern who is telling the truth and to do so without threat or sword. Ironically, a reader who reads via suspicion and looks for the subversive element of the story is wiser than Solomon.

The compassionate reading reveals the subversive nature of the story. One woman is compassionate; the other experiences complete disorientation, even in her response to the king's power over life. The NRSV uses the word 'compassion' to depict the woman's feelings, while the king passes a 'judgment' known by everyone. This interplay of words and ideas suggests two readings after the manner I have presented; one is compassionate and the other is a legal reading.

Subversive readings are suspicious readings. They are compassionate readings, and they look for literary clues within the text to learn the author's intent in telling the story. Subversive readings question the powers and listen to the voice of the powerless. The subversive reading is a 'spiritual' reading because it hears the text as God does in his compassion.

The error of popular interpretations of this piece is the failure to read with compassion from the perspective of the powerless. The deplorable injustice portrayed in this passage has been ignored by generations of interpreters and preachers. How can Solomon portray wisdom when he cannot insure the health and safety of women and children in his kingdom of greatness? Is this story really placed here for us to think of it as an example of wisdom, or is it placed here to offer us an opportunity to hear God's heart and read the historical narratives of Solomon correctly? Like all kings, Solomon's wisdom has been corrupted by his power. Solomon is the state and the state oppresses women and children because it is run by people who seek to dominate others rather than serve.

Acts 4:32–5:16 - Great Grace, Great Power, and Great Fear

The artistic element of subversive narrative storytelling lends itself to literary devices that direct the reader to a suspicious understanding of the story. A 'spiritual' reading might begin with a blanket suspicion on all constructs of power. The intelligent reader might initially uncover the meaning through careful attention to the stories construction. This can be accomplished through use of literary devices such as character development, repeated words, the history of meaning found in phrases, and the overall structure of a flowing narrative that contains specific units. All of these tools are useful in uncovering the manner in which themes of progress and redemptive violence are exposed.

The story of the deaths of Ananias and Sapphira is an example of the power of literary devices to uncover the subversive meaning. I will begin by taking note of the structure of the book of Acts that contributes to understanding the significance of this story in relation to the coherence of the book. First is a simple observation on the three characters that form the interplay between three stories.

In the pericope of Acts 4:32–5:16, Peter is portrayed as both a judge and a king in cooperation with the apostles. They receive monies delivered at their feet, in contrast to Jesus who washed the feet of his disciples. They become the distributors and rulers over 'the company of those who believed'. This phrase sits in contrast to the word 'church,' which will appear for the first time in the book of Acts at the end of this pericope. The word 'church' is introduced when people are filled with fear and refuse to join the apostles because of their fear. These people are the church, while the apostles have become like other leaders, people who inspire fear and lead by utilizing power over life and death. The phrase 'laid it at the apostle's feet' is used three times in this pericope.

The words 'great grace' and great power' are used twice at the beginning of the pericope, and at the end, the word 'great' is used twice coupled with the word 'fear' (great fear). A careful reading understands the grace to have been upon the apostles who in their immaturity did not yet know how to image the son of God. The great power exhibited by the apostles in this pericope is their power over the new community's economics and, in Peter's case, even their lives. The text never states that God is responsible for the deaths of Ananias and Sapphira, and I wonder if this great grace is given to Peter simply because the text does not overtly identify Peter as the culprit who ordered their deaths, yet his complicity in the events is undeniable.

For a moment I will skip the next character and jump to Saul who will attend to the stoning of Stephen. In Acts 7:58 the witnesses who stone Stephen laid their garments at Saul's feet, which should cause the reader to remember how death accompanied the laying of money at the disciples' feet. In the midst of these two persons, Peter and Saul, there is a man that images the son of God in such a way that words similar to those of Jesus spoken from the cross will be found on his lips at his death.

The apostles have become so important that caring for widows is exempt from their practice of faith, they are too important to wait on tables. So, they appoint Stephen, a man full of the spirit. The fledgling movement of Christianity is quickly becoming a power to contend with, using violence and even the death penalty. To lie to an apostle is equivalent to lying to God, and forgiveness is not offered to the offenders. There is no great grace for Ananias and Sapphira, only great power, a power that acts in the name of God and takes their lives without mercy.

Stephen, the first recorded martyr of Christian faith, is strategically placed between two like powers. They are alike because they are both religious powers who claim to speak in the name of God and have power to take the lives of those who would offend them. Their names are Peter and Saul (Paul). Saul's revelation of Christ will change him; Peter's ongoing experience will require his own death.

I suggest that the subversive message of this story challenges violence as an acceptable practice and warns against forming hierarchical structures that exalt some over others. The story also refutes any idea of progress in human governing since the newly spirit-filled apostles fail under the leadership of Peter to exhibit the death of Christ, whereas Stephen the servant of widows was like his Lord.[52]

---

[52] I think it is reasonable to consider that both Peter and Paul are vying for the position of High Priest. Peter will abandon his effort for the High Priest office due to persecution. Paul, the persecutor will abandon his pursuit to become High Priest due to the power of Stephen's death, which he witnesses and which prepares him for the revelation of Jesus on the road to Damascus.

Spiritual Stories and the Deconstruction of Historical Myths

Suspicious of the Powers

Spiritual readings are compassionate, suspicious of the powers, and accomplished through faith in God as merciful. I contend that a spiritual reading of the Bible is accomplished when the recorded stories are thought of as historically rooted myths told for the purpose of communicating theological understanding of the world. With this spiritual lens on history a book such as Samuel (1 and 2) can be read as a theologically constructed myth on the development of the state. The 'myth' is rooted in a real history but told for the purpose of serving as both a history and a subversive narrative that encourages the reader to read with suspicion. The same principle of legal reading and compassionate reading is applicable to the stories of Samuel, although the legal reading might be understood as the state-approved reading and the compassionate reading as a reading of faith. A reading of faith seeks to find God not on the surface of the reading, but ever present in the text as the voice of reason and compassion; not as a warrior, but as merciful; and not just to David, although David seems to need an overwhelming amount of mercy.[53]

The state is not like God; the state wants people to sacrifice their children for its wars and imperialism and for the males who run the state. The state forms its own myths and produces its own heroes of war (rather than faith). The state demands an allegiance that God himself does not. Not only does the state stand in the place of God, but the state exceeds the demands of God on human beings. The state demands the sacrifice of children to the idolatry of its powers.

2 Samuel 2:11-17 - Old Warriors and Dead Heroes

The story of Old Warriors and Dead Heroes is found in 2 Samuel 2:11-17. At first reading this particular story seems completely absurd, like an event removed from reality that could not have actually occurred in the real world of warriors and heroes. The numbers of men involved in the mock battle for the entertainment of generals is twelve from each side. The number is important for it represents the

---

[53] Yhwh as a warrior is promoted through the phrase 'LORD of Hosts'. The Bible's first use of the word 'host' or 'multitude' is used to speak of the sun, moon and stars and is found in Genesis 2:1, where it functions as a polemic against personified cosmologial powers. After Genesis the next use of the phrase 'LORD of Hosts' is in I Samuel, which is the history of the beginning of the nation state. The nation state needs a God that practices war.

number associated with nation-building throughout the scripture. They all kill each other simultaneously, according to the story. Were there really twelve and twelve, or did the event even occur? Why this story? What is its significance, its lesson, amidst the many events that fill a history of war?

A nation of people has been divided into two nations that are at war one with another. They have a history that springs from a single father and mother. They are family. The spiritually enlightening lesson is that we are all from one man and woman and one family, and we are all killing each other in meaningless battles on behalf of governing powers that are in opposition to God's will for humanity.

What might have convinced these young men to come out and put on this meaningless display of heroism? The text does not say, but certain speculative reasons can be given with some sense of reality. The idea of a 'contest' perhaps implies that these young men are ambitious and desire to be heroes, who, like David against Goliath, fight for reward. If so, then they are volunteers prepared to make a name for themselves, in which case they are the competition for the old men's post, specifically Abner and Joab. Abner and Joab's collusive plan is a nice way for old men to rid themselves of rivals.

This idea of a few fighting rather than all-out war has never worked; e.g., the David and Goliath story. The old generals Abner and Joab know this, and their show is but a spark to ignite the battle, and a way for them to secure their power and positions as men who send young men, even boys, out to fight and die. Essentially, they rid themselves of their dangerous competitors.

This story is followed by another with a similar lesson on how dangerous old warriors act in the face of young would-be heroes. In the following story, Abner is being chased by Asahel. Asahel is young and swift; Abner is old and slow. The young Asahel wishes to take the life of a general and make himself a man of power, a hero. Unfortunately for Asahel, he has not yet learned that old men are dangerous and grew old because violence for them became a way of life. Violence is always easy; it requires no real strength or courage or reasoning. It is only violence.

Abner warns the young Asahel to turn aside and take the life of one of Abner's own troops. Abner warns Asahel that he will kill him if he continues his pursuit. The story requires little imagination; it is simple. Abner hears the young Asahel gaining, and just when Asahel is fooled into believing he has worn the old man down, the old man kills him without even turning around to look at him. Abner uses the blunt end of his spear and drives it through the body of Asahel. The lesson is simple: old warriors are dangerous, and they will get young men killed. The death of young men is but a game for them. Young men with their strength and agility should never underestimate the survival instinct of an old man who practices violence.

The Spiritual Quest to Locate God in History

The Bible as a book records God's self-revelation amidst the history of the people of God known as Israel. The quest to locate God in the history of Israel is the spiritual task of biblical interpretation. This quest continues through the New Testament and into the present as we seek to find God amidst a history of violence, war, greed, and intolerable injustice perpetrated upon the weaker members of humanity.

Hide and Seek

The motif of hide and seek begins in the garden narratives. The lesson from Genesis implies that it is not God who is hiding but humanity. It also implies that it is not humanity who is seeking, but it is God. God asks, "Where are you?" and the human beings respond with "I hid myself." This is in accordance with Jesus' perception of God as a good shepherd who seeks even for the least, even for the one. We seek God not because he is lost or even hard to find; we seek him because we are lost amidst a world of violence, pained with the presence of death. Our world is a product of our own uncreative activity that God in his mercy has allowed to continue in order that he might seek and save those who will listen to his voice and respond to his immeasurable mercies. We hide behind our fear of death rather than gain the spiritual impetus to find God amidst human history. God has entered history and interacted with and through a people known as Israel. God has entered history in a visible living image in Christ. We find God through faith in his work in Christ and through the power of resurrection as an event located in history.

It is my assertion that the voice of God in history is not found in that constructed record of those who dominated or 'won'. Even the history of the 'church' is a history of winners that lacks the revelation of God, given to the poor masses of humanity. We need a creative writer to record the history of the church with subversive stories that give voice to the oppressed, the victims of church history. For this reason the biblical record is nearly alone in recording the history that locates God.[54]

---

[54] Howard Zinn compiles a history of the United States through the eyes of the victims of history.
See: Howard Zinn, *A People's History of the United States* (New York: Harper Collins, 2003).

2 Samuel 5:22-25 - Thus Says 'Who'?

Jeremiah and Paul would both assert that the ones who know God should 'glory' in their knowing. To know someone enables you to communicate what they are like. To know God via his spirit enables a person to speak for, or, on behalf of God. Paul would balance this idea with the statement that we carry this treasure in earthen vessels. Thus, no one person has a monopoly on God's voice in the world.

The powers of government and law that rule over humanity always desire to commandeer the voice of God as fully integrated into the state. David understood this when he centralized both political and religious power in his capital city.

Second Samuel 5:22-25 is an interesting little story where David proclaims that Yhwh had spoken to him and had even manifested his presence to direct David's warring efforts. Usually when David inquires of the Lord, he frames his questions to receive either a 'yes' or 'no' answer. This is because he is likely using the Urim and Thummim stones, and tossing stones only gives you a 'yes' or 'no' response. However, this time he is said to inquire of the LORD, and he receives more explicit instructions to bring about his success in battling the Philistines. Understanding that David represents the state and the state commandeers the voice of God for its own purposes helps us to read the story with some justified suspicion. I suggest that this type of spiritual reading is a mature reading.

In this brief story, David claims that as he inquired of the LORD, he was told to attack by coming up through a field of 'balsam' trees, and to attack when the sound of marching came up on the tops of the trees for the wind was the presence of God going before them. It is really quite simple; David has been roaming this country for some time and knows the terrain. He also knows that at a certain time of year and at a certain time of day the weather changes and brings a breeze that blows through a particular grove of trees. The wind then makes enough noise for his men to move undetected amidst the sound and ambush their enemies. David's thinking, planning, and experience do not equal the voice of God. However, David must align his fighting and his reigning as king with God's voice to gain the complete allegiance of his men.

David utilizes religious belief to boost troop morale. He uses his knowledge of the land to play off of the faith of his troops. David makes his knowledge and greatness to be God's. David's deceptive use of religion and his deceit are a portrayal of the state's false construction of reality.

When God Liberates, Look for Mercy

One of the subversive stories in the biblical record is the story of God's self-revelation contained in his battle with Pharaoh. It is subversive because the story challenges all forms of human government that do not know Yhwh, while revealing the character of God amidst an intimate battle with the powers.

The following interpretation is a product of my own reading of the text and in that sense it is original and possibly unique. I share it because as far as I know no one else has offered this reading.

An Interpretive Lens for Reading

Yhwh proclaims his name three times. Initially, he introduces himself simply by the proclamation of the name which he gave to Moses in Exodus 3. In this chapter Moses has ascended up the mountain and God descended to meet him. I suggest that the interpretive lens given to readers in this passage is God's own self-description as merciful. A spiritual reading of scripture or of history must always be a reading that looks for mercy. In all of the Old Testament, Exodus 34 is the seminal text for understanding God.

> 5 The LORD descended in the cloud and stood with him there, and proclaimed the name, "The LORD." 6 The LORD passed before him, and proclaimed, "The LORD, the LORD, a God merciful and gracious, slow to anger[55], and abounding in steadfast love and faithfulness, 7 keeping steadfast love for the thousandth generation, forgiving iniquity and transgression and sin, yet by no means clearing the guilty, but visiting the iniquity of the parents upon the children and the children's children, to the third and the fourth generation." (Exodus 34:5-7)

After the initial proclamation of 'Yhwh,' God speaks his name twice more as though he is preparing to speak about himself. Pondering over his self-appellation and his desire to communicate himself further, he begins his speech. The terms and phrases which God chooses to use to reveal himself and his nature are merciful, gracious, slow to anger, and abounding in steadfast love. These terms and

---

[55] 'Slow to anger' is translated from an idiom 'long nose'. Patience is a better translation. The use of an idiom in a poetic piece suggests the expression is to be contemplated upon. We cannot think of God being angry as comparable to, or compatible with human anger.

phrases are all relational and indicate how we are to understand God and his actions in a world where every event is not filled with clarity.

The speech begins in verse 6 after the word 'proclaimed' and continues through verse 7. The speech is delivered in Hebrew poetry through parallel lines. In verse seven God keeps steadfast love for thousands while simultaneously forgiving iniquity (lawlessness), transgression (violation of the law), and sin (being in a position before God, void of God). As verse 7 continues, there is a sudden change in the presentation of his person. Remember, he began his speech with, "Yhwh, Yhwh, God…" As God, he is the creator and is solely responsible for the realities of existence. God visits the iniquity of the parents upon the children not through punitive intervention. God does not look at a person and decide to bring calamity into his/her life at any given day to cause that person to suffer for the sins of the parents. Rather as creator, God has connected humanity through the ongoing process of generations that go and come through death and birth.

God wants Israel to realize that they are not to live solely for themselves, but are to live for the benefit of those who come after them. If a father is lazy and does not provide for his family, then his children are affected by his actions (iniquity). Usually there are no more than three generations alive at one time that actively have ongoing relationship. Four would be unusual and five would be a rare exception because the oldest member of the family will die before the youngest would know them in a relationally connected remembrance of life.

In his self-revelation God tells us what he is like, and then tells us what it is like to live in the 'space' which he has provided for us. God is a relational being, and he has made us relationally connected beings who affect one another with our words and actions.[56] God's visitation upon the generations is done through the manner in which God has designed our existence together as human beings. The creation of finite beings who are to bear the image of God requires certain realities for existence, all of which are governed over by God. Therefore, the 'visitation' of the iniquity of the parents on the children is not an active intervention by God into human history, but a God-created reality that determines the nature of our

---

[56] To be a self according to Kierkegaard is to reflect upon your self. This reflective practice brings change and produces a newer self (the process of becoming). There is the reflective self, the self that is reflected upon and the outcome is the becoming self. We can only reflect upon ourselves in relation with others. To relate your self to your self indicates that we are relational at the core of our being. Yhwh's reflective action is depicted in the repetition of his name prior to describing himself as merciful, gracious, slow to anger, and abounding in steadfast love. God can only be merciful if there is someone on whom he can bestow mercy. See: Soren Kierkegaard, *The Sickness Unto Death*, eds. and trans. Howard and Edna Hong (Princeton, NJ: Princeton University Press, 1980), 13-14.

existence. The separation of God from creation must be acknowledged in order to know God intimately.

Mercy amidst Plagues

When God meets Pharaoh, mercy meets violence in a battle over the possession of a group of slaves.[57] God is concerned that the Egyptians know that he is Yhwh.[58] The complexity of a merciful and powerful being engaging an unbelieving demagogue is the plot line for the events of the battle over slaves. Acts of power have a way of concealing the mercy of God. However, God is not found in the acts of power, but in the mercy that works in the midst of the powerful acts used to liberate slaves. Power obscures our view of any being whether God or human. Power is like violence; it is easy to use and brings quick results. The will of the powerful one trumps the will of the powerless one.

Moses has been told by Yhwh that he (Moses) is going to be like god to Pharaoh. As a character Moses is like Pharaoh, a god. The scene is simple; two old men appear before Pharaoh, one is 83 and the other 80. Both of them are Hebrews, slaves to Egypt. Moses and Aaron represent an oppressed people viewed by the powerful as 'less than.' When they appear before the commander of all Egyptian forces, they arrive with a stick. Moses and Aaron throw down the stick, and miraculously it becomes a snake. However, Egypt's magicians are capable of performing acts of illusion and duplicate the feat for the eyes of all to see. Although Aaron's staff swallows up the sorcerer's, Pharaoh's heart is hardened by the absurdity that any God would send such a poor spectacle before a great ruler like Pharaoh.

People do not handle power well; they will ostensibly act out of their ego and for their own betterment or preservation. Power always corrupts a human being. In Exodus 7:3, God says he will harden Pharaoh's heart. In Exodus 7:13, the narrator informs us that Pharaoh's heart was hardened, as Yhwh had said. The narrators' announcement comes after the events in chapter 7, verses 10-12. Yhwh's statement in verse 4 and the narrators' in verse 13 form a literary inclusio on the entire episode. God acted in weakness and not in power. God used two elderly old men with a simple shepherd's stick.

---

[57] The idea that God interacts with the state is comprised in the phrase 'mercy meets violence.' God's interaction with the illegitimate reign of human beings over other human beings through coercive force and elitist ideas of governing is always merciful. God's tolerance of the state exhibits his mercy towards all human beings.

[58] This is made clear through the consistent use of 'the recognition formula' which is "…and they shall know that I am Yhwh."

A river of blood. God knows that men like Pharaoh require blood before they will relinquish their power, so God gives Pharaoh a river full. Pharaoh also knows that in a battle a good warrior will seek to cut off the water supply of the enemy. God could have defeated Pharaoh with this singular act, but God did not want to destroy Pharaoh or Egypt. God wanted them to know that he is Yhwh, God of slaves. God's mercy put the Egyptians on their knees digging in the mud like slaves, so that they could find drinkable water. God's singular act of mercy against a potentially devastating act of power is enough to cause Pharaoh to see this 'god' as weak and unwilling to do what is necessary through unrestrained violence, which is Pharaoh's only way of maintaining his rule. Pharaoh hardens his heart against God's mercy, because his pride halts him from relinquishing his power to an invisible God, or an old man 'god' with a walking stick.

Frogs and God's allegiance to slaves. When God assaults Pharaoh with the discomforting presence of swarming frogs that rob Pharaoh of his sleep, Pharaoh attempts to add Yhwh as another god amongst Egypt's pantheon of gods. At Pharaoh's request Moses prays for Yhwh to remove the frogs. (A funny sight: 'frogs in the white house and old men with sticks). That Pharaoh was offering Yhwh a position amongst the Egyptian pantheon is made evident in Moses' reply. The irony is that Pharaoh is offered the power to determine the moment when the frogs will be removed.[59]

> And he said, "Tomorrow." Moses said, "As you say! So that you may know that there is no one like the LORD our God (Exodus 8:10).

In this version of the 'recognition formula,' Moses declines the syncretism of Pharaoh by stating that Yhwh is the God of the Hebrews. This is not an exclusive move, for God is also concerned about the Egyptians. Rather, it is a literary device to reveal the syncretism of Pharaoh's efforts. Moses is not looking for institutional acceptance. He is demanding that Pharaoh recognize that Yhwh is acting to keep promises that he made to the ancestors of the Hebrews. Moses shows himself acutely aware of Pharaoh's ploy in his response. However, the ease at which Yhwh relinquished his hold over Egypt did not exhibit enough force to cause Pharaoh to acknowledge God. Part of the lesson of God's engagement

---

[59] I suspect Yhwh was being offered the position in the Egyptian pantheon as the god of frogs. Rather, God will be known as the moral and merciful God who liberates slaves and acts merciful with a guilty empire. He will be known as the God that wants to teach both Pharaoh and slaves.

with Pharaoh teaches us that God cannot reveal himself through power.[60] God is known as Yhwh outside the constructs of power.

Gnats. The plague of gnats permeates the land like flying dust. This time the Egyptian magicians cannot explain or duplicate the feat. The magicians acknowledge that this act is accomplished by the finger of God. As a leader Pharaoh must show himself strong when those around him begin to falter. God knew that he would act accordingly because he knew Pharaoh, as he knows all people and how power overcomes them. People are not meant to rule over each other; rather, we are meant to serve each other with love and humility by taking on a position of appearing as the weaker one.[61] Verse 19 makes it clear that Pharaoh will not listen to the magicians:

> [19]And the magicians said to Pharaoh, "This is the finger of God!" But Pharaoh's heart was hardened, and he would not listen to them, just as the LORD had said (Exodus 8:19).

Once again it appears that the statement, "…just as Yhwh had said" refers back to the recognition formula. God will not be assigned as one god amongst many. God will not be known as a mere cosmic power represented by the forces of nature.

Flies. In the flies episode Pharaoh again experiences the mercy of God and thinks he is able to 'control' God's actions through Moses. This is the second time during the plagues that Moses has acted with mercy, listened to Pharaoh's request, and asked God to relent. It is important to note that neither Moses nor Pharaoh is actually honest with each other. Pharaoh does not intend to let the people go, and Moses knows he is not going to return after the three-day journey for offering sacrifice to Yhwh.

---

[60] Divine limitation is essential if God is to act redemptively in a world where his will is not done. God's respect to the existence of human beings is such that God will not over ride the human will with his power.

[61] The strengths of Christian leadership become weakness when the demand to bend to the will of the gifted leader becomes the will to which all submit. Self-effacement, attentiveness to the needs of others, and an ear to hear the voice of God amidst life's complications is imperative for the Christian leader. We are to pray for God's will to be done. God's will is not subject to the human tendency to follow the leader.

Pestilence. In this episode the pestilence destroys all of the livestock in the field. Animals housed in stables are preserved as are the animals of the Israelites.[62] Verse 7 reveals why Pharaoh's heart is hardened. It is because none of the Israelites animals were destroyed and Pharaoh has the power to take them all. Once again God does not portray himself as a consummate warrior capable of the type of violence required to be a Pharaoh.

Boils. I submit that the reason Pharaoh does not succumb to the plague of boils is because he himself is not touched by the plague. The text does not explicitly state that the boils come upon Pharaoh. The implication is found when Pharaoh is able to stand before Moses, while the magicians suffering with boils could not. Pharaoh again refuses to see this as an act of God's mercy upon Pharaoh. God does not want Pharaoh's kingdom; rather, God wants Pharaoh to learn what he (Yhwh) is like. In the next plague, God explains to Pharaoh that he has allowed Pharaoh to live that he might reveal his power and introduce his name throughout the earth as a result of delivering the Israelites from Egypt. After this in Exodus 9:14, God states explicitly that he will send his plagues upon Pharaoh.

Hail. In this episode God's revelation of himself is more fully explained through the speech delivered by Moses to Pharaoh. Yhwh is not a good warrior because he tells Pharaoh what he intends to do and gives Pharaoh the opportunity to avoid the loss of any animals that he has left after the pestilence. In this episode Pharaoh's heart is hardened because he knows that the hail has not ruined the wheat and the spelt. Pharaoh can continue to survive and so can his people because of the mercy of Yhwh. The rulers of nations do not surrender easily; most will allow their entire nation to be destroyed and millions of lives in the process before they will abdicate their throne of power.

Locusts. In this episode Yhwh proclaims that he has hardened Pharaoh's heart again. His reason for continuing the battle with Pharaoh has all been for the purpose of revealing himself through the retelling of these events. Pharaoh's officials are prepared to meet Moses' terms; however, Pharaoh is not. He is willing to let Moses and his men go and worship, but not the children (which would

---

[62] The plagues of frogs, flies, gnats, and pestilence all represent the explosion of life from the ground, but it is those creatures that have no benefit to humanity for a stable food source that are multiplying. Further, the livestock are dying because of the pestilence. The connection of humanity's moral and ethical behavior to the ground is portrayed in the life produced from the earth in Egypt. Egypt is full of life, but it is destructive. Pharaoh has roused the moral being that governs all life. Pharaoh's governance is like frogs, gnats, flies, and pestilence.

imply the women also). At this point Pharaoh is willing to offer some dignity to the men in order for them to worship their God. Moses cannot accept such a proposal. Moses has an agenda and does not intend to return.

The plague of locusts begins. Again Pharaoh appeals to Moses to pray for the plague to cease, and again Moses prays and the plague is halted. Yhwh continues to work with Pharaoh and avoids direct assault upon human life. It appears that Pharaoh is learning that Yhwh does not like to kill. However, Pharaoh will require the loss of life before he relents. Like a madman Pharaoh exhibits the tendency of all demagogues to self-destruct rather than face defeat. Yhwh has hardened Pharaoh's heart by taking him to this point. Yhwh is revealed as God over all of nature's power, and Pharaoh is revealed as a madman holding onto power through the oppression of others.

Darkness. This last plague prior to the final act that brings about the liberation of the Israelites is a plague of darkness. Yhwh is still revealing himself and teaching Pharaoh. The Egyptians are in darkness while the Israelites are enjoying the light. Pharaoh summons Moses and is willing to let Moses go with the children. We are told in the narrative that the darkness was for three days. We are not told whether Pharaoh knew that the darkness would last for three days. It appears that Pharaoh did not know. As soon as Pharaoh's heart is willing to release the people with their children, then Moses asks for the flocks and herds also to go with them. At this point the text tells us that Pharaoh's heart was hardened. I propose that when Pharaoh's heart was willing to let the people go, then Yhwh began to return light to Egypt. Then Moses asks for the animals to accompany them, and Pharaoh's heart is hardened once again because (in this case) Yhwh acted mercifully in response to the fluctuations of Pharaoh's heart. Moses departs from Pharaoh's presence with a death threat placed upon him if he ever appears before Pharaoh again.

Yhwh Forced to Assert His Right over Life

This final episode is marked by the act of God killing the Egyptian's firstborn children and animals. Yhwh has been revealing himself amidst human history. He has restrained his power and worked in ways that were intended to teach both Egyptian and Hebrew that he alone is Yhwh God. Moses appears to have delivered his final speech to Pharaoh prior to his departure from Pharaoh in hot anger. When Pharaoh threatened Moses' life, he acknowledged he was ready to kill the Israelites. Moses likely knows that Pharaoh is testing the patience of God by resorting to his threat to kill. Like all tyrants, like all governing presidents, and like all kings, Pharaoh requires the life of his people. He is willing to sacrifice them for the preservation of his continued rule and reign. I have often wondered at Christian parents who are so proud to send their children off to die for the state, yet are unwilling to encourage their children to serve God on the mission field. One of the lessons from the testing of Abraham on Mt. Moriah is that God does not require us to sacrifice our children. However, the state always retains the right to call up your children and send them to any war that the state deems necessary.

Pharaoh thinks of the Egyptians as superior to the Hebrew slaves. Yhwh does not think of them as superior, but as people through whom he intends to reveal himself. Nonetheless, a distinction is made between the Hebrews and the Egyptians.[63] The plague of death selectively took the firstborn of the Egyptians and of any who failed to place blood on their doorposts. The cost of their freedom is blood. Their homes are marked with blood. God himself reinforces the pain of the loss of life by requiring Hebrews, and any that would be saved from the plague to kill a lamb and place the blood on their homes.

Throughout the entire confrontation of God and Pharaoh, God has acted with patience and mercy. However, in order to free the people, God must use force to protect them from Pharaoh by proving himself to govern over both life and death.

God could have destroyed all of Egypt or even killed all the Egyptians. However, he does not do so. Rather, God acts in a way in which he is not comfortable. The command of God for the Hebrews to celebrate the Passover is a perpetual reminder of the cost of their freedom, which was obtained by God's actions against Pharaoh's will. In the biblical story God has killed human beings before (the flood) because they had plummeted into a world where violence filled the earth.[64] Violence against women and children is the crime of Genesis 6. Further,

---

[63] Originally Israel was received into Egypt as honored peoples, guests of Pharaoh. They were brothers and sister to wisdom (Joseph). Joseph had saved Egypt, but he empowers the state and his actions led to the totalitarian system that enslaved Israel. Now, the god of wisdom must teach mercy to men of power. He must reveal Godself because Joseph failed. The promise had passed from Abraham, to Isaac, to Jacob. The promise does not pass to Jacob; he failed. The passing of the promise ends at Jacob, and the birthing of the nation of Israel begins. Yet, Egypt is included in the nation known as Israel through Joseph's sons.

[64] My personal view on this matter is that the writer of Genesis is responding to the surrounding culture with mythical narratives that match the narratives of the other nations. His polemic is to reveal God as Yhwh. His recording of a flood narrative is a re-writing of other flood narratives, in which case the flood remains a mythical event. The message of the flood is not that Yhwh destroyed all of humanity, but that he is merciful and will not destroy us, but provides a promise of seasons and safety under a bow of peace. My thoughts on the flood as a mythical event are reflective of the anthropological reality that all peoples have feared the massive bodies of water that surround them. The geological evidence

Genesis 6 teaches us that men were promoting ideas of racial superiority. The tower of Babel story teaches us that God must increase his governance over humanity to keep us from regressing to a state of corruption brought about by oppression enforced by demagogues and maintained through violence.

This theology should teach us to avoid the empire-building tendencies of all governments. God has not called us to conquer the earth, but to learn to live together without violence. However, as long as human beings are alive (until the end), we will attempt to hold on to power and maintain power by oppressing others, by building empire. For this reason, war will always be a part of human history. Certainly Jesus knew this when he spoke the words, "and you will hear of wars and rumors of wars" (Matthew 24:6). Although it appears that Pharaoh is defeated and the people are free to leave unmolested with the wealth of Egypt, the story is not yet over. There is one more lesson to be taught for the readers of God's subversive narrative history.

Yhwh Reigns and War is Madness

The final battle is the expressed act of an empire's fight for survival. Pharaoh and his people are all guilty of oppression, of injustice, and of failing to honor the image of God in all human beings (no matter how marred). The Hebrew people have departed, and the Egyptian empire is humiliated in its defeat. Yhwh has once again been merciful for he has left Pharaoh with his horses and chariots. Pharaoh's intact army could have served as a deterrent to other people who might plan to overthrow Egypt after their defeat by Yhwh. However, Pharaoh and his people love their comfort.

As Moses lifts up his stick to part the waters of the sea, the Egyptians hearts are hardened to follow.[65] The cry of the powerful is: it is better to die proud than die defeated or live without slaves. Like madmen, they pursue Israel into the waters that Yhwh has divided. The lesson is that war is madness.

The chaotic powers of our existence are all pictured in this moment. We are given a wonderful picture. You can either follow God and live by his promises, or

---

that water once covered the world contributes to this fear. An actual flood is not required, rather the flood teaches us that God will not allow us to fall into the grips of old men who rule over the world, but will deliver us via the founding of nations and languages. War amongst smaller nations of humanity is preferable to the dominance of a few, for they would corrupt the entire earth according to their own uncontrolled lust born of an all-encompassing power. Compare these thoughts with footnote thirty four on pages forty and forty one for greater clarity.

[65] Pharaoh has lost his power to an old man with a stick and an invisible God who aligns himself with slaves.

join the empire and fight for power. Join the empire and you will not survive the chaos of existence. Join God and his people and he will get you to the other side where life and promise is to be found.

Conclusion

Storytelling is not simply imaginative entertainment. It is essential for the communication of truth. An epistemology that does not include subversive narrative storytelling is lacking a key component for understanding the greater questions of life, society, religion, politics, and economics. The Bible is not a book of declarative statements, but a collection of stories that relate the history of the people of Israel for purposes of communicating theological concepts and conundrums. The Bible is not an answer book, but a subversive document that seeks to transform the world.

A spiritual reading of the history of Israel's faith requires close and careful reading of texts with a tenor of suspicion. There is a 'spirit' in the text, or if you will, God is found through a correct reading of the text. The melding of a correct theory with a pure practice should culminate in confirming experience. Experience should inform theory and practice whenever theory and practice need adjusting. Experience is related through storytelling. Storytelling of real life events requires the person recounting the story to do so truthfully. Storytellers can still relate their experience in an artful and subversive manner. This subversive element requires the hearers or readers of the story to bring their hearts into their thought processes. Only a compassionate reading that recognizes God as merciful, gracious, slow to anger, and abounding in steadfast love can correctly uncover the God present in the text.

The Bible is rich with subversive stories. Jesus' speech was particularly subversive. Jesus' stories were often imaginative inventions, yet they were told as such and not presented as real life events; however, their connection with reality was such that they were deeply challenging to his hearers. That a large percentage of scripture would be delivered through stories suggests humanity's need for stories.

Subversive stories communicate a resistance to the powers that govern the world and indicate that God is part of that resistance. The stories that I have presented in this chapter indicate that God is against all use of violence and seeks to establish a people who fulfill the royal law of love with both man and God.

My attempt thus far in this work has been to provide sufficient evidence to warrant a reading of the biblical text that supports the concept of a nonviolent God. I think such a reading can be accomplished with the most testing passages of both Old and New Testaments. I, however, am limited in the scope of my effort. It is my sincere hope that the reader will be challenged to apply some of the interpretive methods I have offered. Like most theologically driven questions, the subject of nonviolence is seemingly an inexhaustible argument between varying opinions. As we stand before the endless wall of eternity covered with the dialectical, theological, and philosophical writings of humanity, the transcendent God of creation rests on the other side. As human beings, as believers in Christ, we find ourselves, like Paul, armed only with conviction against the ever present power of doubt, philosophy's point of departure.[66] It is the power of Christ behind the conviction that validates a life's beliefs.

---

[66] Alan Badiou, *Saint Paul; The Foundations of Universalism*, trans. by Ray Brassier. (Palo Alto: Stanford University Press, 2003), 27. The philosopher Alan Badiou suggests 'conviction' is the power behind Paul's life and service. I would argue that it is the spirit of Christ that empowers the conviction.

CHAPTER 4

A FEMINIST STUDY OF THE FEMALE CHARACTERS PORTRAYED IN JUDGES

My continuing effort to educate my students has required attentiveness to feminist readings of the Bible. This has been so because of the historical tendency of the previous generation's refusal to give women an equal role in the church. This piece on Judges is my own reading. It is based upon my practice to give attention to female characters that are present in the stories of the Bible. I have simply applied this attentiveness to the female characters of the book of Judges.

The following is a theological presentation on one of the greatest problems of humanity, which is the failure of men and women to learn how to live together with one another and before God. Working on the thesis that all violence begins with self-loathing, which is symptomatic of a refusal to act with faith and become spirit, I will argue that humanity is incapable of peace unless males and females learn to live together as God intended. This being said, it is apparent that the domination of the female is concretized in history and the restoration of the female voice requires males and females to learn to live together in a state of mutual respect and particularized equality.[67]

My effort to gain meaning from the book of Judges is limited to the theological instruction offered by attention to the declension of the female voice portrayed

---

[67] By particularized equality, I mean that we must learn to live together, complementing one another's gendered differences. Our gendered state requires learning to understand the other and accept our defined roles as male and female, which are embedded into the nature of life as a result of our physical or bodied differences.

in the women of Judges. The value of Judges as a book is broader than my limited use. Nonetheless, the failure to read Judges without affirming the literary structure that supports a feminist reading is an incomplete reading and will fail to truly grasp the message of the book of Judges.

The theme of violence associated with the oppression of women in spousal abuse and war will promote several statements which I have made previously but need to be repeated. First, once ignited, violence escalates and is only halted by greater acts of violence. Second, when violence escalates to the point of becoming horrific, then human beings stop the violence, but only temporarily; it will resurface. Finally, I will argue that the loss of the female voice in any people will produce a society capable of engaging in genocidal warfare.

Immoral Structures of Oppression

The oppression of women supported by political, social, and religious structures is immoral. The aesthetic dimension of politics inhibits political structures from acting ethically. The aesthetically oriented symbols necessary to maintain a political system are used for controlling the masses and results in unethical practices for the sake of the maintenance of elitism and injustice. The oppression of women is one of the major failures of any political system.

Women are subjected to roles within society that reduce their value to contribute as political, social, and religious beings. They are relegated to attend to tasks which limit their contribution to the social construction of culture. Culture defines the role of women and focuses on their sensuousness while silencing their aptitude for intelligent engagement on the formation of society. The objectification of women and their treatment by the male as a possession, a creature unable to fend for herself, has led to the ongoing development of the macho male.

In the realm of religion women often excel, yet their contribution is diminished and their voice is held at bay and considered to be overly emotional, weak, and unable to face the reality of a violent world. Religion has been used to silence women in every part of the world. Effectively half of humanity has been assigned the role of 'less than;' that is, less than the other half, which is male.

I contend that most violence begins with self-loathing. Self-loathing is a result of a person's refusal to do what is best for others. On the other hand it is willingness, or courage to confront one's self and not attempt to hide the sins and failures that mark one's life from one's self. In the thoughts of Paul Tillich, "Courage is self-affirmation 'in spite of,' that is, in spite of that which tends to prevent the self from affirming itself."[68] When a male refuses to take on the challenge of becoming a human being fully integrated into the male/female world, one result is his tendency to reject the 'voice' of the female's challenging and different experience of reality. The male's rejection of the female results in a self-loathing that must silence the challenging reflection of self found in relation to the female. In other words, the male projects his own weakness upon the female and because of his own self-loathing silences the female voice in the world.

I will make a few statements to clarify my position on the current state of male/female relationships in the church. God is a moral being. We are created with a moral conscience. If the oppressive practices of patriarchal interpretations result in the victimization of women, then all systems of church practice that display and maintain the oppression of women are carnal and are not spiritual.

I consider the oppression of women by the male to be an act of cowardice and power. The Bible portrays the creation of woman in such a way as to link her to the man; meaning that she is from the man, like the man, and not inferior to the man, only different. The presentation of woman to the man by *Yhwh* is expressive of the woman's presence providing what is lacking in the man's need for a kind, loving, procreating, and helping companion to interact with in the world God created.

In the Bible's creation stories the first cowardly act of the man is to blame the woman (and God) for his failure. Interestingly, the woman blames the powers of chaos portrayed in the serpent, yet her reason for partaking of the fruit is reflective of intelligence and wholeness. She partakes of the fruit because it is good for food (an ethical decision over against God's prohibition); the fruit is pleasing to the eyes (an aesthetic reason); further, the fruit of the tree is to be desired because it holds religious value (to make one wise). This being said, it is clear that the woman exhibits existential struggle and rational thought during her encounter with the serpent at the tree. Her failure is she disallows the voice of God found in the prohibition. However, she is but one half of humanity, and her male partner is at the tree with her.

I think that the portrayal of Adam and Eve at the tree is instructive for us on human behavior specifically male and female relational behavior. Why does Adam not speak? Is he inhibited by the intelligence and sensuousness of Eve? Do males oppress women because they fear the smaller, physically weaker, and intelligent female? I am sure that the failure of men to teach women or to deprive them of education is reflective of the male fear of the female's mental faculties.

Further, I think we fear their sensuousness because we refuse to become spiritual creatures who are able to control the desires of the flesh. Flesh desires ease and

---

[68] Paul Tillich, *The Courage To Be* (London: Yale University Press, 1980), 32.

comfort; the flesh does not want to submit to faith's demands for spiritual growth. Building upon the thoughts of Kierkegaard found in *The Concept of Anxiety*, I will explore the codependent nature of male/female relationships in relation to becoming *qualified as spirit*.[69]

Kierkegaard asserts that the sensuousness of women leads to an increase in anxiety; he then explains that anxiety can only be overcome by faith's move to become spirit. So, the male's perception of the female's weakness is, rather, an impetus to move her to become spirit. The female's weakness is actually a point of decision, a point for her to make the move to become 'spirit'. The male is moved to become spirit through love for and acceptance of the woman. The male must choose to hear and accept the woman and in this relational act of love becomes 'spirit'. The creation of woman is descriptive as fulfilling a need in man. It is unhealthy for the male to be alone; the male needs to love the woman in order to be healthy. The woman, however, is prone to independence, as is displayed when she stands before the tree and does not speak with Adam. Adam's instructing, loving voice could have kept Eve from the fruit of the tree, but Adam was intimidated by the woman's sensuousness and intelligence.[70] Eve's failure to communicate her feelings limited her influence over Adam to her sensuousness. Basically, men need to love women and women need to be loved, and love is a giving of self for the sake of the other.

The failure of Adam to communicate with Eve and image God with words of instruction resulted in their failure to properly fulfill their relational role as male and female. The fall of Adam (humanity) was inward and existential. The fall of Cain was external and acted out against another (his brother). The fall of humanity is first inward violence against the self (self-loathing), and then it is outward and projected against the 'other.'[71]

Prior to beginning my exploration of the feminist message of Judges, I will present a number of feminist interpretive practices that I will employ in my reading of Judges. Feminist readings require an awareness of subversive intertextual devices. Feminist readings also require a morality free of imposed readings that are the product of less imaginative minds which seek to dominate females with oppressive readings. Feminist readings spring from the ideology that God is not an oppressive male figure. Healthy feminist readings do not limit the image

---

[69] Soren Kierkegaard, *The Concept of Anxiety*, trans. by Reidar Thomte and Albert B. Anderson (Princeton, NJ: Princeton University Press, 1980), 25-73.

[70] The text offers no reason for Adam's failure to speak. My claim that Adam is intimidated by the woman's sensuousness and intelligence is a reasonable claim. In every culture female sensuousness and intelligence threatens male dominance.

[71] The condition of humanity is depicted in the garden story and as myth serves as an eitiology for explaining why things are the way they are.

of God to gender. A healthy feminist reading honors the voice of (all) humanity. Feminist readings understand women to be the guardians of life and that they are ever seeking life and promoting peaceful living. A healthy feminist reading is a moral reading and liberates humanity from hatred of self.

Reading Judges as a Study on the Declension of the Female Voice

Achsah the Vociferous Woman, Judges 1:12-15

The book of Judges begins with the activity of warring for the pursuit of land. The violence of the Israelite males is justified as retributive punishment upon the Canaanite king Adoni-Bezek. The entire effort is supposedly accomplished in the name of the God of Israel. Inquiries to Yhwh are limited by questions that require either a yes or no answer. The inquiry is accomplished through some stones.[72] The misuse of the Urim and Thummim reduced the reality of God's voice to reading some rocks. The practice had become comparable to our modern coin flipping. The person who uses quick hands to replace a real coin with a coin that has identical sides always wins; he gets what he wants.

The first glimmer of hope for life and peace is portrayed at the beginning of the book of Judges through the voice of Achsah the daughter of Caleb. Achsah is initially portrayed as a prize of war and is to be given in marriage to the man willing to conquer a city for her father Caleb. Caleb's nephew rises to the task and wins the right to marry Achsah. Achsah is as expendable as money and can be used by Caleb as payment and incentive for ordering a man to act with violence and win him a city. Achsah is referenced in the text by name. She is contentious in her relationship with both her father and her new husband in spite of the socially constructed powers of men and violence that govern her life. Like other self-determined women of the Bible, Achsah is agile, strong, outspoken, and concerned with life. Achsah dismounts from her donkey to contend with her father for suitable land.[73] She had asked her husband to request of her father a field; however, her husband fails to do so.

---

[72] The Urim and Thummim stones were placed just below the shoulders on the priest's ephod and were used to inquire of the LORD. Such inquiries were limited to yes or no responses and indicate that there was some method for determining a yes or no answer via the stones; see Numbers 21:21; I Samuel 14:41.

[73] In Genesis 24:64, Rebekah slips from a camel to greet Isaac. In 1 Samuel 25:23, Abigail dismounts from a donkey to greet David, and preserves her household by aligning herself with the powerful David.

Achsah pleads with her husband to ask her father for land, and when he does not ask, she saddles up a donkey and pays a visit to her father. The text allows for the reader to feel the building anger of Achsah directed at the men dominating her life. Her arrival is greeted by her father, who perceives that his vociferous daughter is going to require something from him. The Hebrew text depicts her clapping her hands as she dismounts the animal. The clap is to express the aggressiveness of her approach as she moves toward her father. Achsah is seeking a present; she desires land with springs of water at both ends.

Women excel as the guardians of life's continuance in a world of warring, a world dominated by males. In the story Achsah is a present to Othniel, and she submits herself to the cultural constraints of men while maintaining her own dignity as a woman. Although she is given as a present, she refuses to submissively succumb to the erring ideologies of men. Achsah seeks life's needs and asks for the most basic and essential elements for making life in a new land; she asks for land with water at both ends. She speaks when Othniel would not, and displays more courage than he. Although Othniel can fight and take a city, he is afraid to ask for any more from Caleb than the woman he has already won. I think Othniel is like men today who view warring or raiding as an alternative to working the land. Warring is recognized as a vocation by Othniel and a way of providing for his family. Caleb has made the practice of war a bartering tool and his daughter a prize of war. Achsah seeks a land of peace and security where life can thrive without war.

Deborah the Prophetess of Peace, Judges 4 and 5

Deborah the prophetess is the second female character to be introduced in Judges. Deborah's reasoning for calling Barak is not immediately clear. However, verse 9 offers some clarity on the desires of Barak. Barak wants to defeat Sisera, the commander of King Jabin's army. Barak thinks of Deborah as a good luck charm. Deborah calls Barak and orders him to gather troops because he is going to anyway (verse 6). She is a powerless female; her office space is the shade of a palm tree, where she sits judging Israel with wisdom and without war. However, Barak, her opposing male counterpart, seeks to war rather than learn lessons on how the people of Israel are supposed to live in the land. The story is written to instruct the reader on the peaceable ways of women and on the factors that lead women to participate in violence.

Although Deborah appears to be validating warring and confirming Yhwh's participation, her position as a woman limits her engagement with men to subversive activities that comply with what she cannot stop men from doing. Deborah knows that the efforts of Barak will be successful because she knows that a woman is going to take the life of the commander Sisera.[74] The lesson of the story (in part) is instructive on men and war. Men will war in order to make their names great. By aligning himself with Deborah, who is a popular figure of peace, Barak manipulates and draws the religious element into his story. Further, his war effort can be viewed as a battle for peace. If he can kill Sisera, then he will solidify his greatness as a national hero. This would propel him into a place where both religious and political symbols of power belong to him.

A battle ensues, and Barak's troops are overcoming Sisera's troops. The commander Sisera flees on foot. The life of the commander, the general, the president, the king is always more valuable than his troops. It is not considered cowardly for a commander to flee, but it is cowardly for a foot soldier. This type of duplicity is seldom questioned by those persons deceived by the power of political propaganda. A foot soldier would be put to death for desertion during war. The text offers the reader to view Sisera as a cowardly man seeking shelter from a woman.

Like Achsah, Deborah the prophetess lives in a world dominated by men and must survive and seek to preserve life amidst the violence of war. Her seeming complicity in the violence of war is subject to a nationalistic interpretation of events. Deborah is a victim of political powers. Deborah and God are both misunderstood and suffer the association of their names with war.[75]

Jael the Female Assassin, Judges 4:17-22

In the process of fleeing, the cowardly commander comes upon the tent of a woman whose husband is not present. Jael knows the commander and comes out to greet him. The only information in the text that would explain Jael's knowledge of Sisera is the word spoken by Deborah in verse nine.

> ⁹And she said, "I will surely go with you; nevertheless, the road on which you are going will not lead to your glory, for the LORD will sell Sisera into the hand of a woman." Then Deborah got up and went with Barak to Kedesh (Judges 4:9).

---

[74] In the story, Deborah knows the heart of Barak, and she knows that Sisera is going to fall at the hands of a woman; see Judges 4:9. The story of Deborah must be interpreted in concert with the feminist message of Judges, which is revealed through the development of female characters and their decline from Achsah to the nameless concubine.

[75] If Israel wins, then God was with them; if they lose, then he was not with them. In our current age we do not like to talk about the losing, but we do associate God with our victories. The state usually attempts to justify warring with the accepted religious faith of the people.

I suggest that Jael knows that Sisera has been delivered into her hand. Perhaps she has heard the word of Deborah, or at least the composer of the story uses literary design to lead to this proposal. The woman comes out to comfort the fearful and fleeing commander. She wraps him up in the rug in which he hid. Sisera asks for *water* from Jael. Thinking structurally about the female characters of judges, the request for water should remind the reader of Achsah's aggressive behavior to obtain land with water from her father. Jael brings him milk. The text is confirming the place of women as guardians of life. Milk is representative of life's ongoing cycle from birth to death. Jael will attend to the death of Sisera. He has moved from a wrapped blanket, nursing at his mother's breast, to be wrapped in a rug and rendered dependent upon the kindness of a woman who offers him some animal's milk. Sisera attempts to command Jael by asking her to lie about his presence. I suspect that Jael used her beauty to draw Sisera into her tent. I suspect that Sisera thought she wanted to associate herself with a powerful man.

Jael does not access any weapons to slay Sisera. She uses tools that are made for setting up a tent, a home. Tucked away like a baby, wrapped in a rug, and fed warm milk, the exhausted commander falls asleep. Jael uses a hammer and a tent peg to bring an end to the life of a man responsible for the warring practices that threaten life. Jael nails Sisera's head to the ground like a tent cord.

Barak, in pursuit of Sisera, is greeted by Jael. He finds Sisera dead at the hand of a woman who uses tools designed for putting up her home to kill the commander. Barak's efforts at heroism are halted by two women. Deborah rides with Barak and deprives him of solitary heroism, and Jael kills Sisera and deprives Barak of the heroic notoriety he would have won for killing Sisera.

The song of Deborah and Barak is wonderfully subversive. Verse 4 of the song (that fills chapter 5) suggests that an earthquake and rain was used by Yhwh to throw Sisera and his army into a panic and flee. This is in accordance with verse 15 of chapter 4.

> [15] And the LORD threw Sisera and all his chariots and all his army into a panic before Barak; Sisera got down from his chariot and fled away on foot (Judges 4:15).

Verse 7 of the song praises Deborah as a mother in Israel, and verse 8 suggests that forty-thousand people did not possess a weapon. In the end of the song Jael is praised for her slaying of Sisera. Barak is not celebrated as a hero, and the women Deborah and Jael, in their weakness and as guardians of life, are accredited with working in heroic ways.

An Unknown Woman Saves a City, Judges 9:50 – 57

This particular passage of Judges is interesting on multiple levels. This is so because the story is built upon two established motifs: nation-building and a murderous brother.

> [24] This happened so that the violence done to the seventy sons of Jerubbaal might be avenged and their blood be laid on their brother Abimelech, who killed them, and on the lords of Shechem, who strengthened his hands to kill his brothers (Judges 9:24).

That Jerubbaal (Gideon) has seventy sons is remarkable and instructive for understanding that Gideon, like Jepthath, is an early portrait of Israel's coming kings. Gideon's sons number seventy, and the number seventy is indicative of a nation.[76] The sons of Gideon have been slain by their brother Abimelech whose name means my father is king. Abimelech's ongoing campaign to establish himself as a king is to be short-lived.

After destroying Zalmon and its entire population, he salts the ground so that nothing will grow. Abimelech's conquering is without any concern for the continuance of life. He kills people and destroys the ground. This act makes him a murdering figure who surpasses the role of Cain who is cursed from the ground. Abimelech destroys the ground intentionally. The ethical and moral behavior of humanity is connected to the ground, and this is taught throughout the First Testament. Abimelech will not suffer this disciplinary work of God for he destroys the ground as though he were god. Abimelech is the picture of a man who thinks himself immune from God's curse on murder and acts in madness by salting the ground. In his efforts to establish himself as Israel's king Abimelech's expansionist warring brings him to Thebez.

In fear of Abimelech's murderous assault, the people of Thebez seek shelter in a tower within the city. Abimelech proceeds to burn the tower as he had done previously in Zalmon.[77] However, this time an unnamed woman drops a millstone on his head and crushes his skull. Abimelech, the bramble of his surviving brother's parable, loses his life to a woman.[78]

---

[76] Genesis 46:27 numbers the children of Israel who entered Egypt to be seventy.

[77] Today similar mad men threaten all of humanity with nuclear annihilation in order to hold onto their power to rule over everyone.

[78] The function of this parable is to depict all ambitious men seeking to be kings as the bramble of humanity. See Judges 9:8-15:

Abimelech represents the dominating powers of men that establish their reign over humanity. Humanity is captured in a tower, confined in a city, and the myth of royalty is about to set them all to the torch (like the bramble of the parable). A woman decides to kill Abimelech; her weapon of choice is a millstone. A millstone is used to grind grain. It is a kitchen utensil used for preparing food. Perhaps we are to think that she packed lunch as she sought shelter in the tower and brought her tools for food preparation with her to feed her children.

In the book of Judges, women are placed in positions where they are pushed to use acts of violence. When they act with violence, the weapons they use are wisdom (Deborah), tools for putting up a tent to live in (Jael), and now a millstone (a nameless savior of humanity captured in a tower by the man who wanted to be king).[79] Abimelech's macho response to his ensuing death is a request to be put through with a sword so that it will not be said that a woman killed him. This attitude is reflective of the oppression of women practiced by the dominating powers of governing kings. It is also reflective of the madness of a man to think that it is important that their historical myth be maintained after their death.

This story is also reminiscent of the tower of Babel. Cities and towers are representative of the male tendency to govern over the rest of humanity through the accumulation of wealth (the city) and the practice of war (the tower). To view the tower as representative of all humanity captured by the conquering power of the bramble of humanity is instructive. The message is that humanity is saved by the guardians of life, by a nameless female; she represents all women. We do not hear her speak, and Abimelech attempts to silence her voice when he orders his armor bearer to kill him, rather than have it said that he was killed by a woman.

---

[8] The trees once went out to anoint a king over themselves. So they said to the olive tree, 'Reign over us.' [9] The olive tree answered them, 'Shall I stop producing my rich oil by which gods and mortals are honored, and go to sway over the trees?' [10] Then the trees said to the fig tree, 'You come and reign over us.' [11] But the fig tree answered them, 'Shall I stop producing my sweetness and my delicious fruit, and go to sway over the trees?' [12] Then the trees said to the vine, 'You come and reign over us.' [13] But the vine said to them, 'Shall I stop producing my wine that cheers gods and mortals, and go to sway over the trees?' [14] So all the trees said to the bramble, 'You come and reign over us.' [15] And the bramble said to the trees, 'If in good faith you are anointing me king over you, then come and take refuge in my shade; but if not, let fire come out of the bramble and devour the cedars of Lebanon.'

[79] This story suggests that humanity needs women to save us from the violence of men. Particularly, within the book of Judges, it suggests that the restoration of the female voice is essential for peace. The unsuspecting power of a woman to act salvifically with violence is forced upon women. Violence is not as easily aroused in women as in men.

The narrator of the story refuses to let the male will to establish the myth of war and superiority display the final word.

The Righteous Daughter of Brash Words, Judges 11

Jepthath, the offspring of a prostitute and the illegitimate son of Gilead, is displaced to the land of *tob* (good) and lives free of his half-brother's covetousness over the family inheritance. Jepthath survives as the leader of a gang or a raiding party. Jepthath is portrayed as a rejected brother and son, a man who is forced to make his way in the world without family. The elders of Gilead are cowardly and need a man like Jepthath to deliver them from the assaults of the Ammonites.

After forming an agreement with the elders of Gilead to become their leader, Jepthath demonstrates a degree of diplomatic intelligence in his speech to the Ammonite king. At this stage the story is optimistic about the character or ability of Jepthath. However, it becomes apparent that Jepthath's education about Yhwh is limited, and he understands God to be Yhwh of Armies, a conquering God who delivers up land and cities to his people. For Jepthath, the contest is between the god Chemosh and Yhwh; for this reason he makes a vow to Yhwh to insure his victory over the Ammonites.

The lack of the knowledge of Yhwh and Jepthath's inexperience in religious ideologies results in a vow to gain Yhwh's favor.

> [30] And Jepthath made a vow to the LORD, and said, "If you will give the Ammonites into my hand, [31] then whoever comes out of the doors of my house to meet me, when I return victorious from the Ammonites, shall be the LORD's, to be offered up by me as a burnt offering" (Judges 11:30-31).

The vow suggests that Jepthath is willing to sacrifice a person from his own family or household in order to secure his victory.[80] The willingness to lose a person from his house suggests Jepthath wants to demonstrate to others that war is costly in human lives, and he also is willing to suffer the cost. This would make his vow a feeble attempt to make himself equal with the people (Deut. 17:20). A thinking person realizes that Jepthath would warn his daughter of his vow in order to preserve her life. Jepthath's daughter, however, has her own reasons for insuring that she is the first 'thing' out the door upon her father's return from his victory over the Ammonites. She is aware that the firstborn is not accepted by Yhwh as a

---

[80] To suggest that Jepthath had animals roaming freely around his home is inconsistent with the story's function to teach; rather, Jepthath is willing to sacrifice a human life, a life under his care. This suggests he is seeking self preservation and considers Yhwh to be interested in ritual sacrifice as acceptable for gaining God's favor.

sacrifice, but is to be redeemed.[81] The structure of Judges around female characters suggests a perspective that validates the actions of the female to preserve life. It is notable that, like the previous woman, Jepthath's daughter remains nameless. Her awareness that she can be redeemed according to the law allows her to preserve the freedom of any of Jepthath's household slaves. She, however, will become a redeemed sacrifice to Yhwh and will be as dead; she will not produce any children. She understands that her father will fulfill his vow. She spends two months with her friends before becoming a woman set aside in the house of Jepthath as a sacrifice.[82] Jepthath's only hope for descendants (in the story) is his daughter. Jepthath's experience was that he was the son of a prostitute who had to sell her body to live. It appears that Gideon has not instructed Jepthath in religious belief, a difficult task when you have seventy sons. Jepthath's mother was an oppressed woman and unable to properly educate him. His daughter will never bear any children because of his failure to understand Yhwh. Jepthath is a victim of male promiscuity and oppression. He fails to understand his own daughter in spite of being raised by a woman.

She will never 'know a man.' She will never bear any children. She will sacrifice herself to preserve the slaves of Jepthath's house from her father's brash words and stubborn heart. Jepthath's vow was made to preserve his victory and return to his home. His daughter will sacrifice herself in order to preserve the life of Jepthath's slaves. She will spend two months with her friends, and the text offers a picture of women weeping upon the mountains over barrenness imposed upon a woman. She will live out her life in her father's house as a preserved memory that represents the costs of vows made by warring men.[83]

---

[81] Exodus 34:19-20:

> [19] All that first opens the womb is mine, all your male livestock, the firstborn of cow and sheep. The firstborn of a donkey you shall redeem with a lamb, or if you will not redeem it you shall break its neck. All the firstborn of your sons you shall redeem. No one shall appear before me empty-handed.

[82] The bewailing of her virginity suggests an imposed barrenness. The suggestion that barrenness could be imposed upon a woman by a powerful man is consistent with Michal's experience as the wife of David.

[83] The right of women to bear children is taken away by the loss of life sacrificed to the state through the warring of men. The women wailing on the mountains represent the weeping daughters of humanity everywhere who are deprived of children because the King (or President) has taken the life of one of his slaves as a sacrifice to the god of war.

Yhwh Speaks to a Barren Woman, Judges 13

It seems that God is on the side of barren women and opens their wombs. The story of Samson's mother, the wife of Manoah, is the story of a woman to whom God speaks with and for whom he opens her womb. The angel of Yhwh also charges the woman to raise the son she will birth. This is interesting because it suggests a woman can do a better job of raising a son than a man. Unfortunately, the nameless mother and wife loses her voice to her husband. She shares with her husband the words of the angel of *Yhwh* (a theophanic appearance).

Manoah seeks to hear from the angel of Yhwh himself. The messenger of Yhwh appears again to Manoah's wife. She runs to get her husband, and he asks questions of the 'man' (angel or messenger). The LORD responds, "Let the woman give heed to all that I said to her." The angel of Yhwh repeats all the words that had been previously spoken to Manoah's wife. Manoah desires to control the events unfolding between the angel of Yhwh and his wife.

Manoah's wife does not require the angel's name nor does she ask from where the messenger came. Manoah asks the messenger his name, but is refused. Manoah needs the counsel of his wife to understand that Yhwh speaks to women and even to Manoah. The appearance of the angel in the flames of Manoah's sacrifice convinces Manoah that the angel was in fact Yhwh.[84] This particular story suggests that Yhwh prefers the female's guidance and direction in the son's life over that of the father.

Samson's mother remains nameless throughout the narratives of her life as wife and mother. Unfortunately, it appears that the image of the over-masculanized, or macho male as hero, corrupts Samson. For Samson, women are objects and can be used to fulfill the desires of men.

---

[84] The Hannah story at the beginning of Samuel demonstrates a woman's effort to keep her son away from her husband and leave her promised son with an undiscerning priest (Eli). Hannah in effect raises Samuel through acts and words, by talking to him at the yearly sacrifice, and by making him a little ephod so he can be dressed like a priest. The rearing of a son apart from his father suggests the impact upon a male by a woman produces a better man than one exposed to the dominance over women passed on by males. Elkanah's statement that he is better than ten sons is insensitive and reflective of a macho attitude. Hannah's son must be free from Elkanah's influence in order to be the answer to her prayer. The rearing of Moses by Pharaoh's daughter and the saving of his life accomplished by the midwives (Shiprah and Puah), his mother, and his sister Miriam depict the positive impact upon Moses by the women that formed his life story.

A Strong Man, a Submissive Woman, and a Prostitute, Judges 14-16:3

The narrator of Judges leads the reader to believe that Samson's desire for a Philistine woman is a legitimate ruse in order to acquire a reason to attack the Philistines. Samson's relationship with this unnamed Philistine woman is void of communication. She does not share with Samson the threats that prompt her to coax Samson for the answer to his riddle. Samson refers to his wife as a heifer. Acting in anger, Samson kills thirty men and takes their clothing in order to pay on his wager which he had lost over the solution to his riddle. He returns later to sleep with his wife but she has been given to his companion. Samson's response is consistent with his animal-like strength and nature. He destroys crops and slaughters human beings. Samson's next assault on the Philistine peoples follows his liaison with a prostitute.

Delilah: Loved but Unloving, Judges 16:4-31

As a character Samson is not depicted as wise or cunning. His strength is wasted on women and retaliatory acts of violence on the Philistines. Delilah is only another woman who can be used by men to overcome the strong man Samson. She holds Samson in her power, and the story of Delilah's efforts to learn the secret of Samson's strength is similar in tactics to the first episode where the Philistines sought the answer to Samson's riddle from his loosely held partner.

Religion, Greed, and Israel's Widows, Judges 17

This story depicts Israel's priests as sons willing to steal from their mothers to support their idolatry. The story exposes the oppression of women by Israel's sons. Their idolatry is love for money at the expense of widows. The mother has issued both curse and blessing upon her son. However, the blessing has no value for it represents Yhwh with an idol made of silver from a portion of the money stolen by the son. The birthing of a priestly family is portrayed in this story. Micah makes both an ephod and teraphim to accompany his idol, and he installs one of his sons to function as a priest.

After a while a Levite comes along, and Micah hires him as a private symbol of power and a surety for blessing. The last half of the story portrays unscrupulous men of power as patrons to the priesthood who are reduced to hirelings.[85]

---

[85] Chapter 18 of Judges continues the theme that portrays Israel's priests as hirelings and the priesthood as a corrupt institution controlled by money and power.

The Silent Concubine, Judges 19

This is a story of abuse, cowardice, terror, genocide, and horror, and portrays the trafficking of women as a form of male repentance.[86] The silver idol representative of the priesthood's corruption is a reminder of the curse on male dominated structures that support the abuse of women. This theme (the abuse of women) introduced in the previous section on "Religion, Greed, and Israel's Widows" (Judges 17) is emphasized from chapter 19 to the end of the book of Judges. The idolatry of religious power is utilized by men to justify systemic injustice against half of humanity. The lesson of chapter 18 is that religion is controlled by those persons willing to use the extreme violence of extermination. The Danites warn Micah's servants to be quiet or they will suffer the loss of their lives, and their households will be destroyed.

Chapter 19 begins with the story of an abused woman. She has fled home to her father in an attempt to escape from the priest who keeps her as a concubine.[87] After a four-month absence, the priest arrives to claim his property. The reported joyous reception of the woman's father is a ploy in order to keep the priest at his home for a longer period of time so that he might convince the priest to abandon his desire for the man's daughter.

The father was able to keep the priest in his home for three days based upon simple hospitality. The father uses food and drink to keep the priest for an additional two days. On the sixth day the father is unable to keep the priest. The literary intent of the author suggests that the father did not wish for the priest to take his daughter. The desire of the daughter is not even considered in the text. At this point in the story the violence, associated with priests, suggests that the father is fearful of the priest and unable to stop him. The eating and drinking ploy also supports the idea that the father fears the priest.

The priest departs on his journey with his concubine, and he refuses to stay in Jerusalem because it is a city occupied by foreigners. He travels onward to Gibeah.

---

[86] The trafficking of women as a form of male repentance can be seen in poorer nations due to demasculization of the male psyche because of the effects of colonization and poverty. International economic disparity is overcome by submitting to the dominating group of males by allowing them to abuse the women of the dominated group of males. The existing camaraderie between the dominating males of both groups is established in the mutual domination of the women. In the Judges story, the genocidal act against the Benjamites is a horrendous crime, and its effects on the surviving Benjamites collective psyche is overcome through the mutual conquering of the women.

[87] The word (concubine) *pileges* is used rather than *ishah,* which is indicative of a wife. The charge of abuse will become clearer as the story unfolds and is consistent with the literary tenor of the previous stories.

Unlike the father of the concubine, the city of Gibeah is an inhospitable city, and initially no one takes the priest and his entourage in for the night. An old man responds to the need and offers them a place for the evening. At first the priest refuses because his company has provisions of food. The old man speaks peace to them and requests them to come in to his home rather than stay out in the city square. This story bears resemblance to the story of Lot (Genesis 19) with its themes of hospitality, the danger of the city, and the dehumanizing desires of men expressed through aberrant sexual domination. The old man offers a carousing mob of men both his daughter and the priest's concubine. They seem less than interested in the women and demand the priest. The priest, seemingly fearing for his life, throws out his concubine like a piece of property or an animal to be disposed of as surety for his safety.[88]

In a fit of violence, the crowd mentality of the men results in the abuse and rape of the concubine throughout the night. Raped and abused, the woman is let go and finds her way back to the (hospitality) door of the old man's home.[89] The woman collapses at the door. The priest opens the door to find her either dead or near death. She is laying with her hands on the threshold. It is a frightening picture: a young abused woman, forced from her loving father to be the property of a violent priest. She finds no home; she has no place of solace where she might be treated like a human being.[90]

The priest speaks to her and demands she rise and leave with him. She, however, is either dying or already dead. Upon arriving home, the priest uses her body as an object of horror with which to incite a violent response from all recipients. The priest cuts her into twelve pieces to be sent to the tribes of Israel.[91] The horrific site of female body parts suggests that, if you do not respond, then you will lose your control over women. It is not that the priest cares about the woman. The message is that males must respond to the horrific sign act of the

---

[88] The priest's sacrificial offering is an abused woman. She is treated with less dignity than an animal and offered up to the god of violence represented in the violent act of male sexual domination, which the men of Benjamin were seeking to inflict upon the priest. If you will, the priest's sins are expiated by the sacrificed woman. This nameless woman finds no mercy. God is not reigning in Israel and women suffer the violence of male egos.

[89] It seems hospitality is reserved for males and women are marginally less than human.

[90] The sacrifice of women to the wealth and power of institutionalized religion is portrayed in this story.

[91] Saul uses this same device to warn all who do not respond to his call for war that he will take away their livelihood. The oxen were farm animals, but now they are slaughtered to incite war. Saul's statement is: leave your farms, or I will take away your livelihood.

priest in order to maintain the myth that men are the protectors of women in a violent world. The story also suggests that women are the sacrifices offered for the survival of violent males.[92]

The priest's speech to the rallied troops of Israel suggests that the men of Benjamin are, at least, sodomites that should be slaughtered, and guilty of inhospitable behavior. The priest's ideology suggests that the people of Israel war against Benjamin in order to destroy the similar evils that caused the destruction of Sodom and Gomorrah. The Benjamites refuse to release to Israel the men guilty of the crime in Gibeah.

It seems Yhwh is a poor warrior because the Israelites suffer defeat at their first and second attempts to war against the tribe of Benjamin. Troop morale is boosted by religious symbols (the ark and some priests), and the next assault on the tribe of Benjamin succeeds due to military strategy. The Benjamites' confidence affects their judgment, and they are drawn into an ambush. The escalation of violence culminates in a genocidal assault on the tribe of Benjamin. The Israelite army burns their cities to the ground and kills everyone, except a small number of troops that escape.

In order to support the myth that men protect women, they have labeled the Benjamites as Sodomites, inferior humans subject to complete destruction. This resulted in an oath that forbade them to ever give their daughters to marry a Benjamite. Horrified by their violence, the Israelites stop just short of complete annihilation, and do not continue to pursue the six hundred troops who escaped.

The Israelite's oath had included that any group who did not come up and fight with them would be put to death.[93] The violence continues as the Israelites seek to provide women for the escaped Benjamites. Their solution is to slaughter the people of Jabesh Gilead because none of their people participated in the war effort. Peaceful people are to become sacrifices for the violence of Israel and the survival of the tribe of Benjamin. The Israelites slaughter all except 400 women found to be virgins. The problem is 600 men survived, and only 400 women have been provided. The women trafficked to the formerly labeled sodomites are victims of genocidal violence committed against their city. The Benjamite troops are *guilty victims* of genocidal violence in so far as the need for their continuance is

---

[92] The tribes of Israel are moving towards a united government. It seems that the Benjamites refuse to allow the legal decrees of the larger federation of government represented in the eleven tribes to dictate the extradition of criminals from their territory. The dismembering of the concubine's lifeless body is both military strategy and psychologically supportive of male domination over women.

[93] This is the second time in Judges when men make vows and refuse to repent. Rather, they keep their vows at cost to others, but not to themselves.

based upon the need for females. The excuse to kill entire people groups is usually seen as a righteous act by the aggressors.

In order to provide wives for the remaining Benjamites, the elite group of decision-making warriors arrange for the Benjamites to kidnap unsuspecting women during a religious feast. The elitist group insures the Benjamites that they will convince the fathers that they have not violated their oath, which was not to allow the daughters to marry Benjamites. The violation of the oath is excused because the daughters were taken. The suggestion is that the patriotic thing to do is let the Benjamites have your daughters and be grateful that you kept your oath.

The abused concubine at the beginning of the story remains nameless. She never spoke a word throughout the entire story. Our clearest memory of her is a picture of a woman, abused, raped and murdered, lying at the threshold of a door where men remain sheltered on the other side. As the story unfolded, the violence escalated from spousal abuse to genocide to the trafficking of women as property, and finally, to the sanctioning of kidnapping women as a form of repentance on behalf of the genocidal acts of Israel's elite. The men of Benjamin are preserved because they are men, more specifically because they are valiant combatants. The voice of females is not to be found in the entire story.

Conclusion

The declension of the female characters flows from the vociferous Achsah to the subversive prophetess Deborah and the assassin Jael. The declension continues with the unnamed woman who represents all women, and suggests that men need the female to act to save humanity from the megalomaniac's destructive torch. The story suggests that the redemption of humanity from the conqueror's fire is found in the female gender.

Jepthath's daughter has sacrificed her feminine desire to have children in order to prevent the sacrifice of a member of her father's house. Jepthath's daughter is more humane than her hero father, and renounces his practice of war and his willingness to sacrifice a member of his household to his god of war. Manoah's wife, Samson's mother, was charged with rearing a child for God, but failed because she incorporated the man (unlike Hannah, who does not make such a mistake).[94] Women become victims of the epitome of the macho male (Samson),

---

[94] Hannah desires to have a child for God. She does not want her son to be raised by a man. Her experience with Elkanah and other men in her society is an indictment against male behavior, placed at the outset of the book of Samuel. Although Hannah delivers Samuel to Eli, it is Hannah's visits and words that inspire Samuel and the text portrays Samuel as a child given to God and reared

and are reduced to silent wives and prostitutes. Delilah is the woman who is loved but cannot return love; she is captive to the political powers of men. The mother of Micah represents the decline of the female voice for the males steal from the widows, even from their own mothers. The end of this downward spiral arrives at the nameless, voiceless concubine whose unheard plea is used to promote ongoing violence that culminates in genocide. However, the lesson on violence against women is left unlearned, and in the end women are subjected to state-approved kidnapping for the sake of heroic warriors.

The teaching on women is structurally presented within the literary construction of the book of Judges (whether consciously or unconsciously). The book's instruction includes the understanding that men tend towards violence, while women use violence only when the situation produced by men requires them to do so. Further, they use violence only to preserve life and improvise with weapons from items normally used for tending to the daily affairs of life and peace. The subversive feminist element of Judges focuses on the complete failure of men to learn to live properly with women. The feminist message of Judges is intended to be universal in its scope and guides the reader to think of the stories as representative of the ongoing violence of humanity and the need for women to be liberated from the violent dominance of men. The need for the feminine voice is imperative for peace and essential to halt the warring efforts of men that desire to rule as conquerors.

---

by God. He even sleeps next to the ark of the covenant. As a young boy Samuel experiences God speaking to him and learns to withhold information from Eli. Eli is a poor father and does not rear his own sons.

CHAPTER 5
INTERPRETIVE ADVENTURES IN A CHRISTIAN COMMUNITY A CONCEPTUAL INTRODUCTION

Thus far, in this work, the interpretive practices which I use have been demonstrated with some original perspectives on specific texts. At this point I will clarify in a conceptual fashion the hermeneutical principles I have taught at the Institute for Global Outreach Developments International (G.O.D. International).

First, is the will to find God within the biblical text. This is coupled with an effort to utilize all applicable interpretive perspectives. The result is to form a holistic theology that unites theory and practice into a communal practice. The communal practice is validated through the inclusion of experience as part of the interpretive method. This has been the continuing pursuit of the educational paradigm of G.O.D. International.

The will to find God in an ancient text requires educational preparation that seeks to explore the realities offered by the text from numerous perspectives. This 'will to find God' is the task of theology. Nonetheless, the discovery of 'humanity' runs as a coinherent reality with the search for God. This is so because the limitations of being human require the pursuit of transcendence to begin with the image of God placed in humanity.[95] We understand God in relation to ourselves,

---

[95] When God created us in his image, he related God's self with humanity. We can connect with the transcendent reality of 'Spirit' because we are made to become spirit. We add the choice of faith to the unseen reality of relatedness. God is the object of our faith, and he directs us to center our faith on loving and serving one another.

meaning the revelation of God is found within his creative work. The inwardness of faith moves a human being towards an intimacy with God that is transcendent. The claim to know God is expressive of a transcendent experience and is always accomplished through inward belief.

Although God is separate from creation, precedes all matter, and is self-sustaining, his revelation is accomplished through the incarnation, that is, the Word becoming flesh. God joined humanity in order to reveal himself as both God and as image of God within the confines of the created. God is not found separate from humanity, but in relation to humanity. The external witness of creation cannot connect us to the intimacy of relationship or to understanding of the being or person of God. The internal witness of a moral conscience can only affirm the image of God in which we were created. The self-revelation of God is accomplished as we draw near to him through our being. Theology is supposed to be a spiritual practice incorporating a holistic effort that requires rigorous commitment from the theologian. Christian theology is an ontological exercise on the exploration of human potential as demonstrated in Jesus.

The development of a holistic theology that is consistently applicable to the diversity of theological streams of thought contained within the biblical text is a formidable task. In order to develop a holistic theology, the consistency of interpretive approach must guide the reader, and the interpretive outcome must be consistent with the theological premises that guide interpretation. The development of theological premises that guide interpretation must be correct, or else the interpretive claims will be incorrect. At this point the progressive nature of developing theology precedes the claim to holistic completeness. The interpreter must learn the text, learn about the text, and subject the text to the many interpretive claims made upon it through all applicable interpretive methods, literary tools and reading lenses.

The determination of applicable methods is essential for establishing a valid claim on the meaning of a text. Not all interpretive methods are applicable, nor are all methods reasonably affirmable. For instance, a confessional statement is rich with meaning and useful pedagogy, but it is not as easily subject to a subversive reading or a hermeneutic of suspicion. Some methods are applicable to some texts and yet fall short of being anything other than subjective.

Likewise, the literary development of folk tales for uncovering the origin of a text suggested by Hermann Gunkel is not objectively confirmable by hermeneutical methods aside from comparative literature in the genre of folk tales and a very active imagination.[96] It is the imaginative element that annuls the power of Gunkel's interpretive claims to have any value beyond his own theory. In his

---

[96] See Hermann Gunkel, *Water for a Thirsty Land* (Minnesota: Augsburg Fortress Press, 2001).

effort to reconstruct the formation of the text his claims suppose insight beyond the ability of a scholar so far removed from the actual formation of the text. The detective-like effort of Gunkel is reduced to unverifiable claims. Further, the value of such claims is suspect because they seem to have limited, if any, practical application for the development of a believing community's practice in the world.

The communal contribution to theological development is essential for properly positioning an interpreter. Interpreters who are disconnected from community are unable to affirm the experiential verification of their claims. If interpreters are not positioned within the people of God, they are relationally disconnected from the activity of God in the midst of God's people. The imminence of God in the world requires a theology that is imminent; this is so aside from universal truth claims. An interpreter disconnected from the people is crippled at the task of producing a theology that is applicable to the moment and verifiable by the witness of experience. At the threshold of a biblical text the interpreter serves the community by (if you will) bringing them with him or her. Without the communal connection, the interpreters cease to function in a servant role and become dogmaticians incapable of hearing God.

Not All Texts Are Equal

In the community I lived, I taught my students that within the canon not all texts are equal, but all texts are valuable. The identification of certain texts as primary for theological instruction is born of a familiarity with the Bible and its message. Further, certain texts are given value through repeated use within the canon, or through the streams of theology that are born from a certain text, or simply by the universal power of the text's message to be applicable across time and culture.

God's self-revelation, Exodus 34: 5-7, is one of those texts that gain ascendancy over other texts through repeated use within the canon of scripture.[97] Micah 6:6-8 is the quintessential anti-sacrificial statement and contains the teaching that ritual be replaced with individual responsibility for interaction with humanity. The mythopoeic stories of Genesis 1-11 are masterpieces of literature that reveal psychological and anthropological realities about humanity in both individual

---

[97] The following references to Exodus 34:5-7 are explicit within the canon: Deut. 5:9-10; Deut. 7:9-10; Exodus 20:5-6; Numbers 14:18; Jeremiah 32:18; Nahum 1:2-3; Joel 2:13; Jonah 4:2; Psalm 111:4; 112:4; 145:8; 103:8; 86:5,15; Nehemiah 1:5, Nehemiah 9:17. The implicit references are so numerous that any student of the Bible can verify the primacy of Exodus 34:5-7. Finally, this self-revelation of God is delivered to Moses and spoken in descriptive terms; this passage contains God's own self-perception.

and collective spheres. At the same time these stories offer a theological polemic that challenges the myths of the older civilizations surrounding Israel and reveal the ideology of monotheism.

The addition of passages that would qualify as quintessential to a specific area of theological category are numerous. Philippians 2:5-11, often thought of as an early hymn, provides theological instruction on the incarnation and work of Jesus that is (in the view of many) unsurpassed. Psalm 110, written to preserve the two oracles contained within it, becomes one of the primary Old Testament texts utilized by the New Testament writers.[98] It is this practice of identifying primary texts that begins the interpretive adventure.[99]

Primary Texts and Political Readings

Other texts will gain some ascendancy of importance because the alignment of religious belief and practice has been co-opted to serve the state. The use of religious belief and symbols by the state is done without conscience in order to justify the state's totalitarian practices behind a veil of sacred ideology that supports idols of militarism, materialism and ethnocentrism. The texts used by the state or by the religious leaders that equate the state with God are reduced to religious propaganda. Texts that challenge the state's claim to speak for God will rise to a place of primacy within the religious community that understands the incompatible nature of the state and the reign of God.[100]

---

[98] In my personal study of Psalm 110 and in the course I teach on Psalms and in Hebrew class, I argue that the Psalm was written to preserve verses 1 and 4. The surrounding verses are additions that affirm the oracles with ancient near eastern ideas on conquering. In the New Testament these conquering images become military metaphors for the nonviolent work of Christ. The use of military metaphors to portray nonviolent activity to the early Christians is a common practice of Paul. A careful reading of Paul's use of military imagery reveals a complete dismantling of military practice, e.g. the very symbolic and visible uniform of the soldier becomes unseen traits of faith, character, and practice that adorn the life of a believer.

[99] The identification of 'primary texts' is a task worthy of some effort; however, it is not my purpose here to argue beyond some basic claims that reflect the experience of the theological development of the community of which I am a teacher.

[100] It is my understanding that God will work within the political arena because God is merciful, not because God sanctions the state's right to power. For this reason, I understand the 'community of the King' can work within the political sphere as agents of mercy, bringing God into an environment that will always be hostile to God's reign. 1 Samuel 8 is the 'primary text' that portrays human government as a rejection of God.

The texts that challenge the unchanging status quo of state-sanctioned belief have become part of the theology of the community that I serve. For this reason 1 Samuel 8 is a 'primary text' that guides our reading of other texts and allots those other texts an associative connection with 1 Samuel 8 that forms our theological claims. In our interpretive effort, Deuteronomy 17:14-20 becomes a subtext to the teaching of 1 Samuel 8.[101]

This 'political' reading of scripture becomes an interpretive lens that proves to be applicable to much of the biblical text. The political reading I have taught is a reading that understands the powers of the world to be represented in the false reality formed by the institutionalized and state enervated social constructs of government, religion, economics, science, technology, architecture, and education.

The Bible and the Reader

I often say, "The Bible is only as good as the person reading it." The character of a person capable of challenging a text based upon his/her own sense of right and wrong is superior to the dogmatist who has lost the ability to think critically when confronted with a text that (seems) to support immoral or unjust behavior. A dogmatist is prone to needing a solution for every difficult text, and the need for a solution or answer is not always consistent with the ambiguity of God, life and the biblical text.

One of the hermeneutical efforts of an interpreter is to uncover the intended meaning of the author. Authorial intent is revered by some to be the correct interpretation of a text. However, determining the author's meaning is a complex matter. I often find my own friends and family do not understand me when I speak with the utmost care for conciseness and clarity. To claim certainty on the intent of an author of an ancient text is, in my opinion, absurd. However, it is an important part of the interpretive task to attempt to understand the author. The author's personality might play into his/her writing. The life setting from which the author, the genre used by the author, the textual traditions that informed the author, a search of comparative literature to which the author may have been exposed are all important for trying to understand the author's intent.

The structural worlds of literary works and of the subconscious mind require some acknowledgement of unintended communication. In the case of the Bible, the concept of verbal inspiration would attest to this claim. The truth is we all choose both consciously and unconsciously how we will read a biblical text. Our

---

[101] Many passages in Deuteronomy serve as a subtext to Samuel. The work of the Deuteronomist is a theological redaction that updates past historical texts with fresh theological insights from the lessons of Israel's history.

position in life contributes to how we read a biblical text. Our gender contributes as to how we read a biblical text. Our age, experience, and education contribute to how we read a biblical text.

The will to find God is the practice of theology. The will to hear God is the practice of saints.[102] The disconnect between a purely academic reasoned pursuit to explain the Bible's many passages and a pure encounter with the living voice of God is the perennial tension of the spiritual life for the person who views the Bible as scripture. If the Bible is the foundational document from which all ideology and theological claims are to be submitted, then a holistic theology supported by a living interpretive methodology is required. The problem with my claim made in the previous sentence is the word 'living'. This word implies an immediacy and subjectivity that halts the power of language to reduce the communication of truth to 'bits and pieces.'

This living word is found in the communal voice of a people (the body of Christ) who do theology together and 'hear' together. Jesus claimed that he was the embodiment of truth. The gospel of John references Jesus as the living word; the word made flesh, the voice of God walking in our midst. The interpretation of the word is subject to the living voice. The living voice is actively saying 'yes' in the community that wills to find God and produces saints who hear God. The community that wills to find God in the scripture hears God in the world. The tension between interpretation and application is the holy ground where saints walk. It is the image of God in Jesus that speaks boldly and claims with the pure moral force of his being, "But I say..."[103]

Theology and Revelation

I suppose there will always be a long line of people ready to justify all the words of the Bible with academic rigor. It seems to me that there are only a few who graduate into a spirituality that brings God into the world with a 'new word' consistent with the teaching of Jesus. The existential reality of doing theology has been lost to the dogmatist who desire to stand in the place of God rather than in the place of the Christ. The existential dimension of theological practice is the lived proclamation of a theology that is loosed from a strictly scientific hermeneutic. The intellectual rigor of theological study prepared to wrestle with an idea subjected

---

[102] I use the word 'hear' in the Hebraic sense, meaning that, if you hear you obey. If you hear, you respond with the active 'yes' to God.

[103] See Matthew 5, the Sermon on the Mount, for Jesus' refrain, "But I say..."

to the 'need' of a given historical moment is open to the will to hear God over reasoned dogmatics.

The dialogue between revelation and history is to face reality free of illusions (free of the false constructs of the state). This freedom is to view human history both past and present with revelatory understanding. It is the act of the spirit that enables a person to see the world clearly and honestly. The ability to view history without finding hope is the existential moment when the transcendent reality of God meets the human heart. This loss of hope is the death into which we were all baptized; like the death of Jesus, it is a death to the world. However, hope abides eternal and is removed from the powers and placed into the depths of the human heart. Our hope is in God, and God was in Christ reconciling the world to God's Godself.

Hearing from God is considered to be a revelatory act. The church has submitted all claims to hearing from God to collective agreement on the interpreted word, or to the authority of the ecclesial institution. The ecclesial institution is unlike a community of people who go unrecognized by the state as a formidable political power. I think that every human being has the potential to respond to the voice of God and, through this transcendent event, receive a word from God free from the interpretive task of reading the Bible.[104]

Interpretation makes claims about God based upon rigorous academic exercises. Revelation makes claims about God based upon an experience. The telling confirmation of revelation is played out in the conviction of the person claiming revelation. Conviction is demonstrated in the synthesis of the revelation and the life lived by the person claiming a revelation. If you will, the person who is recipient of a revelation must become the revelation's embodiment. However, conviction is not enough to confirm the claim to revelation. The claim to have had a revelation must be accompanied by both conviction and reason in light of the message of the cross. Ultimately the claim to revelation is verified by a life lived at every moment in light of the revelatory claim. This is the coninherent experience of theory and practice with a lived spirituality.

Revelation Liberates Humanity

Human sacrifice flourishes in the world intended to be the Garden of God. East of Eden human beings seek to hide from spirituality, from intimacy with God. Does the church really believe that human beings are created in the image of God? It seems the church is often more interested in saving that which only God can save (eternity), and does not give enough attention to saving the temporal lives of the suffering masses of humanity that inhabit most of God's world. This

---

[104] See Acts 17:26-27.

tragic shift from the teaching of Jesus and the cry of the prophets has produced a religion that no longer bears or understands the marks of the martyr.

The poor of the earth are sacrificed at the altar of progress, burned (alive) at the altar of war, cast aside like Lazarus, and left as food for wild dogs. The task to liberate the poor from the grips of poverty and the pains of war and injustice is not taken seriously by our leaders, or by the vanity-ridden, publicity-seeking celebrities, or by the church that sits in comfort and is at ease in the world.

Lazarus is at the gate of life and has been sacrificed by Christians in the name of a false peace, a false prosperity, an ineffective faith for which no one is willing to give their lives. We sacrifice our youth to the state and stop them from offering themselves as 'living' sacrifices to the God of the cross (and resurrection).

> [11] And I raised up some of your children to be prophets and some of your youths to be Nazirites. Is it not indeed so, O people of Israel? says the LORD. [12] But you made the Nazirites drink wine, and commanded the prophets, saying, "You shall not prophesy" (Amos 2:11-12).

Inward Liberation

Soul care is a practice that incorporates the psychological with the spiritual in an effort to recover human beings from the pain and sin that has damaged their psyche. This practice is partially accomplished through the development of trust and intense counseling sessions. The truly essential part of the recovery process is the birthing of spirit, the birthing of new life that overcomes the past through the divine love shared by both the minister and the counselee.

The first task is to gain the trust of the damaged person. Trust is not easily earned and requires that liberative workers identify themselves with the oppressed person(s). The term 'solidarity' is helpful to describe the position of the counselor or minister seeking to bring life to the oppressed or damaged soul. Trust is established through works of love accomplished in solidarity. Works of love are actual laborious efforts to improve the living condition of the oppressed person. Works of love also include intensive listening to the cry of the oppressed. God models these liberative efforts because he hears the cry of the afflicted; he seeks justice for the oppressed, and he wants the oppressed to be taught his word so that they might be healed.

Restoring the Voice of Oppressed Communities

The inner voice of a human being is the heart's voice; it is the place where God connects with a person because of his/her faith. Inward liberation is the restoration of the voice of the heart to share in hope and faith with others and God. To listen to the voice of the oppressed in person to person contact is to begin the liberative activity of voice restoration. Inward liberation continues as relationship is developed and trust is experienced.

The liberative servant must gain the trust of the oppressed. The oppressed do not owe you any trust. The dignity of being treated as a human being has been torn from them, and you must earn their trust. The liberative worker is aware that the oppressed person will vacillate from trust to distrust. It is crucial that at the moments when an oppressed person vacillates from hope to despair, from trust to suspicion, that the liberative worker remain in solidarity with them by listening and displaying fearlessness in the face of the oppressive powers. The practice of liberation requires the redemptive suffering of the liberative servant to be offered on behalf of the damaged soul.

Theological Education and Liberation

When the oppressed have been deprived of education, they need to have their mind awakened to the reality of their own power as they take on the challenge to become a human being capable of speaking clearly and accurately about the world. Education on the self revelation of God as merciful, gracious, slow to anger, abounding in faithful, suffering love, and forgiving iniquity, transgression, and sin for generations is essential for introducing them to God. This is wholly demonstrated in the loving act of self-giving displayed on the cross. The liberating power of God's word is to be accompanied by the living agent whose life manifests the ongoing suffering of God.

A Lived Kerygma for Communities of Need in the Philippines

The proclamation of the gospel is more than an evangelistic meeting framed with posters, times, dates, and hype about greatness. The proclamation of the gospel is more than the gathering of people in a building for 'church' on Sunday. It is the 'more than' that I will write about and will use the setting with which I am most familiar.

G.O.D. International's particular calling is mission-oriented with a practical concern for human development and human rights that complements our lived proclamation of the gospel. While serving as the dean of our school, I also trained students to live and serve communities of need in the Philippines. Our spirituality is based upon our interpretive practices which compel us to align ourselves with the will of God in the earth through active participation in bringing holistic liberation to communities of need.

The mobility experienced in our community is indicative of our wealth. Unfortunately, many young people do not have a community capable of teaching young, wealthy heirs of empire how to live with the tension of being a servant of God and an heir of empire. Aimlessly in search of spirituality and meaning, American Christianity supports the massive exodus (not of slaves, but of the citizenry of the oppressive empire) of immature, indoctrinated heirs to empire's power.[105] These young souls are mere purveyor's of paternalism and entitlement, spiritually lacking and underdeveloped; they have nothing to give but tears of pity and promises to forget.

We do not utilize the term 'missionary' on the field because of the grievous meaning associated with the aforementioned activity by some paternalistic efforts. The training required to liberate the heirs of empire from their own ego in order to become incarnated servants sent out internationally is the task now of the G.O.D. community; otherwise, the sins associated with wealth and mobility is our sin and we will weep only for ourselves.

Proclamation and Practice among Endangered Guardians

The first community of need that I will address is the oppressed women of the Philippines international sex industry that preys upon poverty-stricken young women. In search of new language for identifying the 'bar girls' of the Philippines I selected the phrase 'endangered guardians.'[106] The identification of these girls as endangered guardians counters demeaning terms like bar girls or prostitutes. The term 'guardian' is drawn from the concept that women are the guardians of life. This is portrayed in their nurturing and self-sacrificial femininity, in the giving of their body and the risking of their life to birth children into the world.

---

[105] The yearly exodus of young Christians traveling from America to destinations around the globe is a phenomenon born of technology and wealth. It is also a lucrative business for some persons and ministries. It is a sort of amoral practice whose ethical implications have not been explored.

[106] Vandana Shiva, *Earth Democracy: Justice, Sustainability, and Peace* (New York: South End Press, 2005), 139. There are numerous publications that utilize the term 'endangered guardians.' I am using the term in conjunction with the use of Vandana Shiva. The term is established amongst Liberation Theologians and has been used by Pope John Paul II in his Angelus address of July 16, 1995.

The cost of empire and global economic injustice has empowered liminal men to abuse the guardians of life of an entire nation. The girls who work in the bars of the Philippines experience the dehumanizing power of exclusion every day. They carry with them the shame of being known as a bar girl. They carry with them the pain of being reduced to an object of gratification for men, in exchange for a mere pittance to survive. The psyche of these girls is damaged by the powers that imprison them within a merciless system of sexual abuse. As the guardians of life, women naturally tend towards kindness and self-sacrifice. When these attributes of the feminine personality are damaged by the abusive life experiences of a bar girl, she suffers disorientation and lapses back and forth from gentleness and weakness to deception and anger.

This contradictory behavior of the girls is perceived by the liminal male predator to be a mental deficiency due to lack of education and not understood to be the effects of the male's abuse. The male desires the feminine attributes of kindness and nurturing, while tolerating the deception and anger as a defect in the female which justifies the abusive activity of the male.

Male sex tourists are liminal personalities, meaning that they have not experienced integration into their own society. Many male sex tourists are former military personnel. They have been engrained with a sense of machismo and consider themselves to be entitled conquerors reaping the rewards of victory. They view their activity as expressive of their identity and consider themselves to be superior males in contrast to the working, faithful, family man. Other sex tourists are incapable of a normal relationship. They are socially awkward persons whose self-centered existence is built around their needs without concern for the consequences suffered by others due to their pursuit for gratification.

The girls are victims, and the men are the perpetrators. It is the lived proclamation of our community that befriending the girls is the preferential option for positioning ourselves in the world. I understand that when faced with severe poverty and hopelessness, good people will justify immoral behavior. Their immoral behavior is justified on the grounds that the preservation of life is important, and if sacrificing one's morality is the cost, then the decision to commit an immoral act is viewed as positive. The safeguard that qualifies the immoral act beyond the needs to preserve the life of the impoverished group is that the act does not inflict violence upon others. The girls (guardians of life) are guilty of immoral acts, but they are victims of violence. Many of these girls are recruited by employment agencies that sell them to a system that indebts them and subjects them to rape, imprisonment, and isolation prior to entering the sex industry as a worker.

The liminal men commit their crimes from a position of economic and physical power. The affliction suffered by the women is not comparable with the rampant desire of immoral behavior practiced by the men. This being said, the divine love of God for the perpetrator is expressed through the revelation of God working to liberate the oppressed women. As the 'body of Christ' works to liberate the women in the social sphere of human reality, the men witness the light that has shown in the darkness. The revelation of God to the perpetrator is accomplished through the victim.

We all sing the song, "This Little Light of Mine," but most are guilty of hiding that light and refusing to enter the darkness where human beings are reduced to commodities, to refuse, to victims of abuse. Entering a bar to engage nonviolently in a battle against the international sex industry is a lived 'kerygma,' a proclamation of fearless faith, of unquenchable hope, and divine love. A lived proclamation must enter the darkness and practical instruction for engaging in this type of activity is essential for successful liberation.[107]

Bringing Christ to Endangered Guardians in the Bars

> The Son of Man came eating and drinking, and they say, 'Look, a glutton and a drunkard, a friend of tax collectors and sinners!' Yet wisdom is vindicated by her deeds" (Matthew 11:19).

Entering a bar for the first time can be frightening and intimidating for a person raised in a family that participated in a church-centered lifestyle. Bars are loud and are kept dark. The display of young women as merchandise can be painfully shocking. Beer, brass poles, mirrors, half-dressed (or nude) girls on display, loud music, dark lighting, and aggressive males to oversee the disorienting carnival of debauchery is not an environment conducive to conversation or meant for the people of God. In a bar we are intruders, unwanted guests. We need to blend into this unnatural environment, not as participants, but as signs of awareness giving testimony to the love of God for the afflicted. For this reason, workers who enter a bar must purchase drinks for the girls. You do not purchase alcoholic drinks. You can order cokes and in some places juice.

When you ask a bar girl to sit next to you, be prepared for her to be touchy and overly affectionate. She is at work and has compartmentalized her life so that she can act different from who she is outside of this unnatural, constructed environment. You must require her to respect you, and you must respect her. Do not show any physical affection other than a departing hug in the midst of a group. The Philippines is predominantly Catholic, and most of the girls will claim to be Christians. Their wonderful displays of faith and their primordial holiness

---

[107] I submit that the raising of the consciousness of socio-political religious milieu is a part of the liberative task. It is the stories and theology of the liberative servant that communicates the humanity of the community of need.

overcome the depraved environment produced by America's militaristic empire and globalism's economic disparities.[108]

To meet this community of endangered guardians within the confines of the darkness that marks their lives with indelible scars on their psyches and their bodies is to recognize their humanness amidst a false reality that seeks to destroy the image of God that they bear. The lived proclamation displayed by entering the bar demonstrates a solidarity that gives the liberative servant credibility with girls who experience rejection by their own society. Meeting with the girls outside of the bar is the next relational aspect of solidarity. It is by entering the bar that a liberative worker gains the credibility needed to enter into the closed community of engendered guardians.

The lived kerygma is built upon experiences that enable openness to events that are less spontaneous and yet important for building a new community out of the community of need. So, Bible study, times set aside for prayer, and counseling sessions come after the lived kerygma is established as an ongoing part of the less immediate or spontaneous proclamation. For example, connecting events with other human beings are more memorable, more powerful, more given to narrative recounting, when these times take place during lived moments of life's unpredictable power; they provide depth to forming relationships.

I sat in a bar next to a young lady who considered herself to be old at the age of 26, because the average age of most endangered guardians is around 21. The lighting made her eyes look blue (another deception). Initially she continued to sit next to me and speak with me because I purchased coke to drink and small glasses of pineapple juice at cost of $2.50 each. She was given 40 percent of each drink purchased by her customer (me). I shared with her my purpose for being in the bar and my faith in God. She responded, "I do not believe in God; he has never spoken to me." In that moment the spirit of God welled up inside of me and I responded, "God is speaking to you right now. Christ is in me and he wants you to know that he has only forgiveness for you, that he apologizes to you because his church has failed to come and help you, and has treated you as though you were not valued. He suffers when you suffer; he feels your loneliness and your pain; and, like you, he hopes that human beings will learn to treat one another with love and respect." The moment was real and filled with spirit and proclamation.[109]

---

[108] Primordial holiness is a conceptual term used by Latin American Theologians. The term recognizes the ability of the poor to display acts of great kindness and sacrifice amidst severe suffering. See: Jon Sobrino, *No Salvation Outside the Poor: Prophetic-Utopian Essays* (Maryknoll, NY: Orbis Books, 2008), 73-75.

[109] The Columban Priest Shay Cullen has been opposing the abuse of women and children in the Philippines for 38 years. He is the director of the PREDA Foundation, (People's Recovery, Empowerment, Development, Assistance). See:

Proclamation and Practice in Hope's Refuge

> "There was a rich man who was dressed in purple and fine linen and who feasted sumptuously every day. And at his gate lay a poor man named Lazarus, covered with sores, who longed to satisfy his hunger with what fell from the rich man's table; even the dogs would come and lick his sores. The poor man died.... (Luke 16:19-22).

> Again I saw all the oppressions that are practiced under the sun. Look, the tears of the oppressed-- with no one to comfort them! On the side of their oppressors there was power-- with no one to comfort them (Ecclesiastes 4:1).

People pushed to the edge of the city like the smeltering stench of refuse find the power of hope to be their only refuge. They are called squatters and live in slums. I think of them as people of the land, as living in the land of hope's refuge, because the hope of humanity lies in their liberation from the systemic injustices that have led to their abandonment. The city is like a magnet that overpowers the placement of human beings in the world and draws them to itself. The city's immoral treatment of human beings is a reflection of its power to dehumanize both the poor and the powerful until they lose their humanity and their hope. The hope of the city is found amongst persons who have been captured by the city's drawing power and awakened by its false promises. The lie of the city is never more evident than in the midst of the lives of the impoverished that occupy the shacks and hovels of neglect. The hope of the impoverished is ignited by the need to find life while living in the midst of cruelty and injustice. Their hope is for their children to escape the clutches of poverty. This is their primary reason for living.

Life east of Eden is dominated by the powers of those that evade any connectedness with life from the ground. The concrete jungles of Cain are the land where the perennial question "Am I my brother's keeper?" continues to reveal the murderous heart of those who seek security and acquisition of goods over the treasure that is a human being.

The poor of the city are like Lazarus laid at the gate of the rich man. They are left to die of neglect; even dogs are treated better by the wealthy than those whom God helps (the name Lazarus means 'God helps'). The poor know that human beings are more important than animals.

Shay Cullen, *Passion and Power: An Irish Missionaries Fight Against Child Sex Slavery* (Mullingar, Ireland: Killynon House Books, 2006).

Hope's refuge is every slum, but for me it is a particular place in Olongapo City, Philippines. The name of the area is Pag asa in the Tagalog language, and interestingly Pag asa translates into English as hope. A lived proclamation is a community-building activity that unites people in the teachings of Christ, even when they do not know it. Community building that promotes the recognition of the image of God in every human being and seeks to aid communities to be the agents of their own healing through practical acts of love is consistent with the Spirit of God.

The fear that dominates a community of persons whose right to the land that they live on is not recognized by the powers of the state must be removed in order for them to find their voice in a world that ignores the poor. The powers keep those that live in Pag asa in fear through letters that threaten eviction. The liberative agent stands between the poor and the powerful to speak on behalf of the poor and their right to land. It is imperative that our spiritual proclamation of the word challenge the rights of the powers to treat human beings as though they were born into a world that has no room for them.

We are called to advocate on behalf of the landless and use nonviolent methods to insure that they are given land to live on, to cultivate, to build, and to form their own governing bodies from their own community. If you do not have access to a lawyer, then it is wise for the liberative agent to learn the laws and the court systems that govern over others. In efforts to transplant communities it is important to designate persons to pursue a law degree within the nation state that they work. Others need to pursue education in nursing, midwifery, social work, and horticulture. This should be along with completing a biblical education. Biblical education should be a priority and a value for integrating all learning.

The removal of fear brings the voice of the poor to the surface, yet they need to be educated and form skilled articulation on the issues that inflict their lives prior to facing the powers. It is the responsibility of the liberative agent to educate the poor in reading and critical thinking skills, and to recognize and develop their intelligence. The recognition of types of intelligence will aid the liberative agent in identifying and developing the God-given abilities of different persons.

In concert with the removal of fear and the task of educating, it is imperative that the poor take responsibility for their living conditions and be equipped with sanitation education and tools to clean their living area. They are often afraid to clean up their areas, thinking that the powerful will take it away if it becomes an ordered environment of health. The people of slum areas like Pag asa need the liberative agent to assist them in developing their own schools, community gardens, playgrounds, and political representatives. This is the task of a lived 'kerygma.'

Proclamation and Practice with Prisons and Families

> 'For I was hungry, and you gave Me something to eat; I was thirsty, and you gave Me drink; I was a stranger, and you invited Me in; naked, and you clothed Me; I was sick, and you visited Me; I was in prison, and you came to Me' (Matthew 25:35-36).

Jails are always fortresses of violence that separate families and dehumanize their captives (inmates). The systems of incarceration around the world are inconsistent with the redemptive activity of God. Jails are miniature cities where human beings govern over every aspect of another's life and movement.

One of the theological teachings found in Genesis is that families separate in order to stop violence from erupting. This is demonstrated through the story of Abraham and Lot's parting. The quarreling between Lot's people and Abraham's people will result in violence, and Abraham prefers peace and loss of the better land over the eruption of violence. Jacob will separate from his father in-law Laban and set up an 'international boundary' between his family and Laban's in order to insure peace between them and avoid the violence that the text deems inevitable if Jacob remains.

Moses' solution to keep peace and give an opportunity for life to continue for society's offenders was to develop a system that utilized 'cities of refuge', a city set aside for those persons who had committed or were thought to be guilty of some offence. The advantages to Moses' system are numerous. People are not treated inhumanely, but are given the opportunity to form a society with other offenders. In Moses' system the family can join the offender and are collectively given a chance to redeem the past. The effects on the families of an incarcerated person are seldom factored in to the damaging statistics listed on the subject of jailing.

The privatization of the prisons in our society has produced a for profit system of incarceration that requires a legal system to feed the ongoing pursuit for monetary gain. The victims of such practices are always the poor and those who are victims of racism on a societal scale of entrenched social sin.

In spite of the cruelty of imprisonment, the Philippines has made real efforts in recent years to improve the humanity of their jails. This improvement is in areas where liberative agents have challenged the overcrowding and unjust practices of incarcerating the poor, children, and the detaining of persons for extended periods without due process. If there are no challenges to the injustices, then the inhumane conditions of the jails increase.

Entering a Filipino jail is done every day by persons claiming to 'have a jail ministry'. My thoughts and practices on bringing a lived proclamation to the inmates of the Philippines has a number of weighty differences from the common evangelical practice. First, the prisoners need food, soap, and anti-fungal cream. I have taught my students to bring these items along with a book to catalog the names and stories of the prisoners. I also have them bring small bags of rice for the guards who suffer inadequate wages for their time, and suffer the atmosphere of the jail on a daily basis.

The families of prisoners suffer, and so it is important to visit their families. When the liberative agent is without money he/she can clean the yards, fix the house, work in the garden, and teach the kids. After visits to a prisoner's family, the bond between the liberative agent and the prisoner is dramatically intensified; genuine love, trust, and care produce an emotionally connective friendship. Advocacy with the local court can also be productive. Learning on the job is inevitable regardless of educational preparation.

Born Free: The Right of Tribal People to Live Unmolested

Abraham rose and bowed to the Hittites, the people of the land (Genesis 23:7).

The first inhabitants of the Philippines are known as Aeta or Negritos. One of the first locations where the Aeta settled over 5,000 years ago was Mt. Pinatubo. Life on Pinatubo was rich with the bounty of a triple canopy rain forest, natural hot springs, and a habitat suitable for hunting and gathering. Aeta people are less than five feet tall.

In 1997, the Philippine government signed into law the Indigenous Peoples' Rights Act which gave the Aeta title to ancestral lands in various locations throughout the Philippines. Although the Aeta have resisted assimilation into larger Philippine society, recent catastrophes have endangered their tribal lifestyle.

The Aeta suffer the cruelty of racism in Philippine society. They also desire to live unmolested from the modernism and technology that permeates the Philippines. They are victims of land-grabbing elites and corporations. Corporations will build a million-dollar resort at a hot springs on Aeta land, and ease their conscience by providing small housing villages that consist of 300 square foot homes made of cement block with hot metal roofing.

The Aeta need people to help them organize their tribal distinctiveness with written records that enable them to govern their own land free from the invasive demands of a society that is alien to their hunter-gatherer, small farm lifestyle. The Aeta need liberative agents who stand in solidarity with them and their right to be born free and remain free to live their lives connected to the ground that they love.

Exploited Labor

The debasement of the Filipino worker by multi-national corporations seeking cheap labor and large profits has produced many communities of exploited laborers. South Korea's Hanjin Corporation, located on the Subic Bay Metropolitan Authority (SBMA) (the former U.S. military base) next to Olongapo City, is one of the corporations that seek profit over care for their workers; that is, when their workers are Filipino.

One of my first encounters with the exploited Hanjin worker was at an ATM. The young men were paid via electronic crediting, but had not learned how to operate an ATM machine. Another encounter was on the SBMA at the housing provided for workers who were brought in from IloIlo and were going to school to learn to be welders. However, these young men were shipped in because they could be exploited. They had to leave their families; they spoke a different dialect, and were unfamiliar with the dynamics of a powerful corporation and a city.

These young men need people to aid them in developing a community that can protect its interest from the predatory nature of corporate profit. They were underpaid; they had burn scars on their arms from welding without proper protection, and their working conditions are often unsafe. They need their families; they need adequate housing and workers' rights to hold the corporation responsible for work-related accidents that leave them disabled. They need a proclamation of Christian faith that is demonstrated through solidarity and acts of love that liberate them.

Conclusion

The will to find God is a theological task worked out with the word and wisdom. The will to hear God is a spiritual task not subject to reason or requiring an interpretive solution for every difficult text. These two are not exclusive of one another and should be harmonized. The essential practice is the willingness to live Christ in service to the poor and speak openly about injustice in service to all.

The proclamation of scripture is a task for a community; the formulation of a theology applicable to God's concern for justice and the establishment of his peaceable reign must also be done in community. The proclamation of scripture is not just an exercise for Sunday institutional meetings; rather, it is a lifestyle of spirituality that takes to the streets in vessels of flesh the reality of God. The proclamation of the word can take place in a bar, on a mountain, in a prison, and in a slum. The proclamation of the gospel is the light of communities that gives witness to the reign of God by their existence as people set apart to live subject to the rule of God. The proclamation of the gospel is accomplished through a community of people who live as suffering servants who do not resist the persecution of the state when their allegiance to God comes into conflict with the state.

CHAPTER 6

Spiritual Formation in Community: Church Renewal and the Role of Character

Caught in the Paradox of Life
Struggling to Live
While Living without Struggle
Thankful for Simplicity's Smile

by Mike Garner

Introduction

Working in a youth movement has made me the interest of a number of persons that study contemporary church culture. At Lee University I was considered an emergent church leader. At the time I was not even aware of the emergent movement. My life with my students at G.O.D. International was simply the outworking of events that were greater than me. My practice for living and ministering was to do the best that I could. I considered church renewal to be the manifestation of a hunger for God amidst phenomenological responses to cultural changes.

I grew up in the Pentecostal movement whose growth and cultural dynamics I have witnessed in Asia, Africa, Latin America, England, and the United States. I participated in the Jesus movement in the early seventies in California. I was present at the early stages of Calvary Chapel when services were held in a tent. Calvary Chapel and the Vineyard Churches were, to me, just the ongoing phenomenon of people in pursuit of Christ. When I attended seminary in the nineties we were required to read books about the second reformation.[110] All of this has made me think of the church as an ongoing work, a fluid movement able to flux with cultural constructs. The truths of Christianity are not new; they are explored by the generations amidst the unfolding of life and history.

The subject of renewal evidences the hunger people have for more of God. This hunger manifests in many ways and in all types of churches. The church and its continuance is, first, in my thinking, a work of God. I share my thoughts on renewal with my students and have included a section on those thoughts in this chapter.

I have placed this chapter in the midst of a poem. The poem serves as an inclusio to express the tension of our existence and the beauty of life's gift. I grew up in a denomination where the Pentecostal pursuit to return to the spirituality of the first century church was presented as an ideal expression of Christianity.[111] This pursuit was accompanied by a desire for signs and wonders. I have enjoyed my share of signs and wonders. I have also learned to value the realism that enjoins paradox and ambiguity. For much of my life, idealism and the desire for confirming signs and wonders was a constant part of my experience.

In this chapter I will present some of my thoughts on the proposition that the church ever experienced a time of ideal existence. I will also place the phenomenon of signs and wonders within a constructive theology for understanding their purpose.

I will explore briefly the spirituality of Jesus and contend that spiritual persons bring God into every aspect of life, even the darkest places where God is absent.[112] Then I will present a case study of the prophet Jeremiah as a model for mature spiritual formation. I will suggest that Jeremiah's spirituality demonstrates the same walk of faith lived out by Jesus.

---

[110] See: William A. Beckham, *The Second Reformation: Reshaping the Church for the 21st Century* (Houston, TX: Touch Publications, 1997).

[111] See: Robert M. Anderson, *Vision of the Disinherited: The Making of American Pentecostalism* (Peabody, MA: Hendrickson Publishers, 1979), 40.

[112] The absence of God is troubling for persons who hold firmly to God's omnific attributes as static realities beyond the control of God. In Hosea 5:14-15 God is accredited with the warring violence of the Assyrians, and then God declares he will go away and return to his place. I suggest that God is not a prisoner to God's omnific attributes. The absence of God is expressed in scripture as God's hiding of his face. See: Craig C. Boyles, *The Conflict of Faith and Experience in the Psalms: A Form Critical and Theological Study* (London: Sheffield Academic Press, 1988), 73-76.

Hope is an indomitable power in the world and is faced with an indomitable opponent; the ensuing struggle is the formation of reality as we seek to live before God. I contend that hope in the face of life's most strenuous trials is evidence of spiritual formation. I will follow with a short story on character and conclude with a section on the church as an alternative community.

Renewal

It is a cursory reading of the New Testament that promotes the idealistic notion of a time of romantic perfection where believers lived out their faith with purity of heart and exceeded later followers of Christ in spiritual formation. Nonetheless, it is this type of reading that gave birth to the Pentecostal movement that now embraces the world. Romantic and idealistic claims promote the idea that the beginnings of the church were an exceptional time free of human error and failings. However, we are all called to face the difficult task of living out Christ in a world where pain, suffering, and injustice abound. Bad things happen to good people.

The call to return to a time of innocence wherein leaders were given authority based upon the grace of signs and wonders often references the early chapters of the book of Acts. The classic passage for this exercise is found in Acts 4, and particular focus is placed upon verses 32-35. This social experiment is born of enthusiasm, and the practices are, in part, a failure of the early church's leaders to give guidance to well-meaning believers.[113] The Jerusalem church will later become economically without recourse to internal financial resources due to the practice of selling their goods to maintain a common purse under the control of religious leaders.[114] The apostles are reigning over the people like kings, and the money is placed at their feet. What a mess: money, power, grace, and human beings who do not know how to respond to the enthusiasm of the moment.

In Deuteronomy 15 Moses promotes radical but reasoned legislation for the alleviation of debt and the halting of unending appropriation of wealth and power by a few. Moses accepts indebtedness as an incontrovertible reality which must be regulated by law because individual human conscience will not suffice. Moses does not forbid indebtedness; however, he protects people from perpetual debt.

---

[113] My reading of the Ananias and Sapphira story utilizes literary and structural modes of interpretation (pages 63-66). Imperfection or failure to achieve utopian results is inevitable until the reign of God is fully established at the return of Christ. The early church made mistakes, as did the church throughout history and into the present.

[114] See Romans 15:25-28.

Moses' view on economic justice is that it requires access to capital for the needy and protection of the needy from the greedy. Moses halts the accumulation of immeasurable wealth, and if he were alive today, I suspect he would be a proponent for capping personal wealth and opposed to unethical practices of international corporate franchises. I also think he would insist on access to interest-free loans for persons who do not own a home or land and seek to keep them free from indebtedness.[115] Perhaps his land reform would insure that every person born is entitled to a plot of fertile ground on which to build a home and raise a family.

Paul corrects the erring generosity that supports irresponsible behavior in 2 Thessalonians 3. In verse 10 Paul commands that irresponsible people who do not contribute to their own welfare and that of others with honest work should suffer hunger, or at least not be allowed to take advantage of the goodness of the church's charity. Paul's own aversion to indebtedness is exemplified when he insists upon working with his hands rather than receiving monetary support from the people to whom he ministered the word of God. Paul's concept of debt included an arena outside the financial realm, and yet he would draw the financial realm into the moral. This is exhibited in the letter to Philemon. Paul claims that the debt owed to him by Philemon surpasses any monetary loss that Philemon may experience through Onesimus' absence.

Perhaps we will always have the poor with us (as Jesus stated) because we will always have greedy people, or perhaps because natural calamity and illness will strike. Perhaps Jesus knows that we will continue to war and warring inflicts poverty upon its victims, whether they be an overtaxed populace or a defeated enemy. The struggle to alleviate poverty in the world is ongoing and a people without debt display discipline. Yet without the incurring of some debt, buildings for churches, Bible colleges and other religious institutions would not be able to exist in our society. 'It is more blessed to give than to receive' translates over into the need to find a way out of the goodness of your heart to forgive the debt of those that owe you money.

The time of innocence after the Resurrection and Pentecost reflected in the enthusiastic practices of the first followers of Christ is quickly extinguished by the failing of leaders easily distracted with money and power, leaders that behave like

---

[115] The building of a home presupposes that the home will be owned. See Deuteronomy 22:8 "⁸ When you build a new house, you shall make a parapet for your roof; otherwise you might have bloodguilt on your house, if anyone should fall from it." The owner is also held responsible for insuring the home is safe for both inhabitants and visitors. The possession of the land by the Israelites includes home ownership. See Deuteronomy 6:10-11.

kings rather than servants. It will be awhile before Peter becomes the man who can be grabbed by the belt buckle and led around.[116]

The signs that followed Peter attest to God's grace that works with us in our weakness and immaturity. In the early chapters of Acts, there is no record of Peter countering the fame that was attributed to him due to the miraculous signs that followed him. Paul's problem with miraculous signs and his manner of dealing with misdirected attention is evidenced in Acts 14:11-18. Whenever a person is miraculously healed, it is the grace of God at work, and such an event is not meant to glorify the person who prayed for the healing. I suggest that without the signs that Jesus did, very few persons would have given him any attention. So, the signs were to bring awareness to his person. They were an essential yet problematic part of Jesus' life. Further, the *spirituals* of 1 Corinthians 12 list the *manifestations* of the charismata of healing in the plural, so that each act of healing is to be understood as a gracious act of God, and not a power bestowed upon a human being. Likewise, today, as in the time of Peter and Paul, miracles are signs and acts of grace that are meant to arouse the recipient or observers to the message of the word.

Although the church as an institution and as the organic or spiritual body of Christ needs to identify and face its many failures and sins, it is unwise to suppose that there was a point in the history of the church which expressed wholeness and was the ideal era. Some suppose that the new age of technological communications has now enabled the church to reach the world with the gospel and make the work of God dependent upon technological advancement.

Challenging the socially acceptable or status quo in the sphere of ethical and moral behavior is a greater task and has more impact upon life in a positive or a spiritual manner than the progressive development of humanity's ability to build machines that fly. The mythic faith in technological progress is addressed in the proto-historical narratives of Genesis with clarity for all that seek to understand the basic realities of the human family, society, and government.

In these stories that we look to as the word of God to us, we are challenged to recognize that the impetus of invention and technological innovation for building and the arts is all accomplished by the line of Cain. The man that kills his brother is responsible for producing the first city, the first metallurgist, the first artisans of music and crafts. The line of Abel has been murdered, but Seth takes the place of Abel in Adam's line of descendants. Seth's accomplishment is Enoch, (his great great great grandson) the man who walked with God, whereas Cain's is Enoch (his own son), the man after whom the first city is named. It is interesting that the

---

[116] See John 21:18; Peter is told that he will eventually change to a man that is not self-willed and strong, that age will take him to a place where he will submit to the challenges that God will require of him.

name Enoch is generally understood to mean 'initiate.' The story is telling us we can initiate technological advancement in our effort to avoid the hostility of the world, or we can learn to walk with God. Walking with God is more important and more powerful than technology's grandest achievements. The mistaken trust in technological innovation to bring about a better humanity is as idolatrous as a Christianity that trusts in political systems to manifest the Kingdom of God.

I do not want to be misunderstood; technological innovation is not intrinsically immoral. The problem lies with the beings who use technology. I am certain that God has created us to be aesthetically inclined ethical beings who find fulfillment through religious practice. Religious practice is to aid us in our search for God, to draw near to the image of the one that created us, to develop a *spirituality* that allows us to be spirit before we are drawn into the power of aesthetic desire or ethical decision-making. This effort to become spiritual persons is the impetus of religious practice. However, humanity has often reduced spirituality to disciplines with an outward appearance so that others will know. These practices or signs include pilgrimages, clothing, public prayer, symbols whether worn or acknowledged with prominent placement in our homes and public places. The most problematic effort to demonstrate spirituality (in my thinking) is monasticism. Granted these dedicated servants of God did some good, such as preserving, copying, and translating manuscripts. However their ability to be exemplars facing the challenges of family, work, and normal social relations is nullified by their exclusionary spirituality. Unfortunately, all human efforts to produce a spiritual people will be fraught with weaknesses.

Although Jesus chose to remain celibate and unmarried, I see a number of valid reasons that attribute to Jesus' choice. First, Jesus' self-awareness and knowledge of his death made marriage an unwise choice.[117] Second, the burden carried by his possible offspring would have been disastrous due to his uniqueness as 'Son of God'. Finally, sexuality is foreign to God as a genderless spirit and is not essential for human development, wholeness, or spirituality. Jesus demonstrates this truth for all those persons who are victims of a world where they do not find a covenant partner with whom they can produce a family.

---

[117] Jeremiah does not marry because of impending war, and does so as a sign act to accompany his advice that marriage is to be avoided during time of war. Jesus' awareness of his impending early death makes marriage an unwise choice. Jeremiah will encourage marriage once the killing is over.

Spirituality

Jesus is our exemplar; he is the one that models for us the true meaning of spirituality. Since I am writing for Christians, I believe it is fair to claim that Jesus epitomizes the highest lived spirituality obtainable by a human being. Due to the limiting powers of particularity within creation, Jesus' life does not face every obstacle to spiritual living that persons face in various times of human history. For instance, Jesus did not face the ethical dilemmas of parenting in the twenty-first century. However, he did face the cruelty of military domination as the member of a conquered and subjugated group of people. Jesus' experience as a human being in many ways exceeds ours; this is so because he lived out what it means to be human without succumbing to desires that might seek temporary relief through violence, deceit, or uncontrolled lusts of the flesh.

As our exemplar, Jesus is mistaken for a ghost or spirit because he walked on water, but the text makes it clear that Jesus is flesh. Human beings are meant to become spirit while celebrating a life within the boundaries and particularities of creation's limits. Walking on water is a sign and not a feat to imitate. Peter cannot do it even with an invitation and Jesus as a partner.

I think that the proto-historical story of Enoch, the man who walked with God, invites us into a history of human beings that learned to become spirit (only a spirit can walk with a spirit). Their stories are replete with both successes and failures. Jesus aligns himself with these persons who live a life of faith, particularly with the prophets.[118] Jesus affirms the human effort to find God. God is a spirit, and faith connects us to God. Faith or belief is the first move towards spiritual formation. Although Jesus is Lord, he acknowledges the story of other human beings who sought to become whole human beings by, if you will, becoming spirit.

A human being who is spiritually formed or mature is a person who has benefited from interaction with God in other human beings. Perhaps this is best exhibited in the life of Jesus through his association with John the Baptist. Jesus' love for his forerunner is exhibited in his baptism, an act of humility which sanctions the ministry and baptismal practices of John. I do not think that this statement need exclude the concept that Jesus' baptism can also represent his repentance for societal sin. As a Jewish male, Jesus partakes in the benefits of being

---

[118] It is interesting to note that in the context of the story of Israelite history, the first person to be called a prophet is Abraham. This is so because the story of Abraham is about the faith walk of a man. I think Moses understood the concept of prophet to be consistent with God's desire for all, which is that we would all experience God's presence in such a way that we speak words consistent with God's spirit (see Numbers 11:29).

male in a patriarchal society. In this sense, Jesus is guilty of societal sin, without being guilty of disobedience before God or any base personal sin born of the lust of the flesh. We are victims of sin in numerous ways.

Spiritual formation does not occur in a social vacuum, although solitude plays a role through testing and the development of contemplative thought. Spiritual formation is synonymous with imaging God. God is a relational being; this being said, imaging God requires that we be relational beings. A spiritual person may be a misfit and awkward, but will love people. Love of the other is essential for any growth as a spiritual person.

Spirituality is lived amidst a world of human beings who do not know God and is exhibited in the person who brings the presence of God with wisdom and mercy into every situation. Spiritually formed persons do not hide from the world but enter in and dirty their hands through identification with the less than saintly everyday persons of the world.

Jeremiah: A Case Study in Spiritual Formation

Jeremiah is a spiritually developed person whose formation and ministry took place within the dynamics of various communal influences. Jeremiah learns of *Yhwh* without the religious powers that determine what it means to be a worshipper of *Yhwh*. In Anathoth, Jeremiah is the son of a priest, a member of a group of people who have suffered the injustice of being denied access to gain their living via rites and rituals at the temple.[119] Jeremiah's spiritual formation takes place within an environment that was not his choosing. He will later reflect upon his life and understand that his personal spiritual formation was a product of both communal influences and providentially the work of Yhwh.[120]

---

[119] In 1 Kings 2:26-27 Solomon banishes Abiathar to Anathoth and brings to pass 1 Samuel 3:10-14. The passage is understood to mean that the descendants of Eli will not partake in priestly duties. The priests that lived in Anathoth were rejected from temple service. If Jeremiah is a descendant of Eli, then God's 'forever' does not always mean forever, or the Hebrew words translated as 'forever' are contextually understood and not subject to the English word 'forever.' Further, the irony that out of Eli's or Abiathar's lineage God would call Jeremiah is indicative of God's mercy and not the political finality that people try to attach to families both to destroy and to establish myths of 'royalty.'

[120] I understand Jeremiah's call narrative to be a compilation of experiences over the course of his life that he has reflected upon as an older person and written out for our instruction. See: William L. Holladay, *Jeremiah 1; Hermeneia; A Critical and Historical Commentary on the Bible* (Philadelphia: Fortress Press, 1986), 23-32.

Jeremiah's theological education consisted of a story that left him outside the halls of power. His knowledge of foreign lands and animals is but informational confirmation of his education; the truly dynamic phenomenon that highlights the insights of Jeremiah is theological and experiential. Jeremiah's temple sermon is the defining moment in his prophetic calling and reveals a matured stream of theological thought that is capable of imagining a new covenant.

It is important to note that Jeremiah is not seeking renewal, but he is going to attest to the complete abolishment of the sacrificial system and the rites, rituals, and symbols that define Mosaic religion. Jeremiah's understanding of religion is that it is established inwardly within a human being, and that moral living in relation to others surpasses any form of ritual or ceremony. In my opinion, the role of Jeremiah as a religious reformer is theologically unmatched by any other biblical person except for Jesus.[121]

In both Jesus and Jeremiah, it seems that the spiritually formed person's vision for humanity is free from the constraints of power exhibited in institutional religious practice. Jeremiah seeks to establish his efforts at 'renewal' to an idealized moment which is held close to God's heart as a romantic memory. The moment that is extolled in God's memory, particularly by Hosea is Israel's willingness to follow God into the wilderness.[122] However, Jeremiah recognizes the moment when God first called Israel out of Egypt as she ventured out to follow Moses into the wilderness as more complex than a simple romantic memory. Jeremiah understands Israel's first covenant to be: hear God's voice and obey, the same requisite at which Adam and Eve failed. Hosea's contemporary the prophet Amos, in a God speech, will question the veracity of the moment when Israel followed God into the wilderness.[123] Amos will contend that the idealized moment exists only as a hope and not a reality.

Jeremiah will seek to link his theology with written pieces of Israel's story in a manner that builds a solid argument and a present hope. The spiritually formed person recognizes the idealized moment as a reality in the heart of God, a reality to which we are called. But like the fictitious garden story, innocence is not a state in which human beings can develop into matured spiritually formed beings.

---

[121] John the Baptist's greatness is in relation to his historical moment as the voice of the one who announces the arrival of the Messiah. His theological contributions are minimal.

[122] Hosea 9:10 reveals the conflicting element in the romanticized or idealized moment. The idealized moment exists in the heart of God; however, it was not established in the heart of Israel. Rather, the complexity of life, culture, and human action hinders human beings even when they exhibit moments of faith.

[123] Stephen references this verse in his sermon; see Acts 7:43.

Jeremiah's formation takes place within an environment where terror, horror, and the complete demolishing of all that forms Israelite culture and life will take place. Jeremiah is prepared to guide Israel into exile, into a life where the only remaining 'remnants' of Israelite life will be a few people with the story of their faith.

Jeremiah accepts his role as a prophet and a victim of history. Jeremiah is a misfit, a man that finds no value in all the symbols that form the identity of his people. For Jeremiah, it is only 'the word' or 'the story' that has value; everything else is 'hevel.'[124] We human beings are always uncomfortable with those persons who live independent of symbols. We are further troubled when such people begin to deconstruct our symbolic world.

Symbols are esthetic representations of an idea, possibly even a truth. However, symbols are easily commandeered by slogans and are ethically powerless. Jeremiah knows that God brings life out of Aaron's almond rod (staff) and that God watches over his word to perform it. The only thing in life that is certain (outside of death) is God's word. God's word, like Jeremiah, is complex and demanding, ethically challenging, and spiritually awakening.

The associative thinking of the people that made Yhwh and the temple (Israel's grandest symbol) synonymous Jeremiah identifies as a deception, a lie. This word of Yhwh delivered by Jeremiah at the temple gate comes at the beginning of his prophetic service and is preceded by Yhwh's desire to dwell in this place. While 'this place' includes the temple, it does not exclude any location or part of the land known as Israel. This is portrayed in two aspects of Jeremiah's 'temple sermon'. First, Yhwh desires to dwell with the people. His presence is living, and so it connects with the living and not a house of stone. Second, Yhwh sees all that goes on outside of the temple area. God is concerned with every aspect of life, and there is no separation or compartmentalization into spheres of secular and religious. A spiritually formed person brings God into every area of life and sphere of existence. Jeremiah is such a person.

As a victim of history, Jeremiah suffers the movements of history. Jeremiah will not enjoy a wife and a family; his own dictates from the word of Yhwh identified the historical moment in which he spoke as a time when marriages should not be made. Jeremiah accepts his historical moment and becomes an historical person. People who desire to impact history in a way that reveals God to the world must be people who live with and accept the pain and suffering that accompanies facing history with the word of God. A spiritually formed person recognizes the moment in which he/she lives and speaks words that challenge the status quo of political and religious domination.

---

[124] 'Hevel' is the Hebrew word used often by the writer of Ecclesiastes and is translated as 'vanity.'

Although spiritually formed persons exhibit fearlessness, they do not have to behave in a manner that facilitates their demise. Jeremiah's courage to speak at the gate of the temple and proclaim the words of Yhwh are unmatched until Jesus. Nonetheless, Jeremiah will utilize his friend Baruch to present words given to him from Yhwh. Jeremiah claims he is forbidden to enter the house of Yhwh (36:5). We do not read a God speech with such a command; I surmise that Jeremiah needs to stay alive in order to keep speaking. Jeremiah reflects a spiritually formed human being who rejects religious martyrdom as something you seek after to validate your faith.

Jeremiah exhibits a spiritually matured person throughout his life by his resilient power to hope in the face of rejection, imprisonments, torture, war, and captivity. Jeremiah's personal strength that equips him to endure rejection is a part of his person. The knowledge of Yhwh that Jeremiah has and the acceptance that he experiences in his soul from his knowing God enables him to live without the support of social institutions.

Jeremiah is imprisoned and, with the spiritual tenacity of a prophet, clings to his words without retraction.[125] Jeremiah experiences the abandonment of friends and family (Jeremiah 12:5-6). Jeremiah is tortured and produces a poetic piece that is similar to Job.[126] Jeremiah is branded a traitor for encouraging fighting men to offer a non-violent response to the invading Babylonians (Jeremiah 21:8-9). Jeremiah is taken captive to Egypt by his own countrymen, men that refuse to hear the word of Yhwh (Jeremiah 43:1-7). Through all of his struggles, Jeremiah never loses hope in the mercy of God. It is his hope and trust in God's mercy that enables Jeremiah to pen the new covenant (Jeremiah 31:31-34). It is Jeremiah's hope that moves him to perform a sign act and purchase land for family members after him when the Babylonians are going to destroy the land (Jeremiah 32:7-14). It is Jeremiah's hope that calls the exiles to pray for their enemies and captors, to pray for the peace of Babylon, and to live there and marry and build houses (Jeremiah 29:4-7). Jeremiah's spiritual formation cannot abandon hope in the

---

[125] Jeremiah 15:19 records a moment when Yhwh challenges Jeremiah to recommit himself to the word of Yhwh and speak without variance. It is an intensely emotional moment when the man Jeremiah in all his humanness speaks of the paradoxical ways of the world. For Jeremiah, knowing God is not glorious but troublesome because he can find no peace. Jeremiah's confession is directed to Yhwh. We are privy to the interaction. We learn that even the strongest amongst us finds his or her ability to endure through faith in God. So, Paul can proclaim that he can do all things in Christ.

[126] Jeremiah desires to bring his case before God, which is a major motif in the book of Job as Job wants to bring God into the court of human understanding. Jeremiah is tortured at the hands of the priest Passhur; see Jeremiah 20: 1-3. Compare Jeremiah 20:14-18 (Jeremiah's response to Passhur's act of torturing him on the stocks for a night) with Job 3.

midst of the most horrific obstacles. Jeremiah is like his God; hope abides forever; hope is inextinguishable as long as a person is spiritually connected with God; hope truly springs eternal.

Jeremiahs' sign acts sit in contrast to the rituals performed within the temple area. The symbolic ritual is capable of instructing the observer if the observer can translate the ritual's origin and meaning outside of the limiting confines of religion into everyday life. Jeremiah's temple is the world and his rituals are metaphorically rich. Their meaning is easily translated into reality; this is so particularly with Jeremiah's accompanying explanations or words of Yhwh.

For the spiritually formed person, life is a stage where every scene teaches truth to those whose eyes are opened. It is not urgency that drives the spiritually formed person, but love for God and people. There is no greater task than revealing God to others. It is, however, fraught with both joy and sorrow; joy over those whose eyes are opened and sorrow over those who close their eyes and stop their ears.

The simple images of a potter's shop, where clay is spun into shapes and forms, and ovens, which bake the final product to serve its purpose, all become a picture of God and world for Jeremiah (Jeremiah 18:1-6). Jeremiah's ceremonious gathering with the Rechabites lifts from obscurity a people neglected and looked upon as misfits for their separatist practices. He demonstrates out of the Rechabite's loyalty to family and clan, particularly to their founding father, the ability of people to be loyal to God and honor him as the one who forms reality and our lives (Jeremiah 35). Their founding father's commands and voice is still heard, practiced and honored; they receive blessing from Yhwh through Jeremiah. However, Israel has not listened to God's voice or obeyed his precepts and commands, and so the judgments that God has pronounced against Judah will not be averted.

I often think that Jesus had Jeremiah in mind when he invited us to take 'his' yoke upon us (see Matthew 11). Jeremiah's yoke represented the reign of the king of Babylon, but Jesus' yoke is voluntary submission to place ourselves under the reign of God. A yoke represents servitude, and yet Jesus invites us to voluntarily place upon our freedom a restraining instrument that allows another to lead us.

Individual rights and freedoms must be governed by the reign of God, and God's reign asks for our voluntary cooperation in the exercise of life. Freedom without restraint results in unbridled passion and insatiable desire. Freedom requires that human beings limit their own freedom to the welfare of others and the will of God. Christ came to set us free from the excesses of freedom's power that draws us into self-destruction.

During the time of Jeremiah, Israel exercised unbridled passion and tested the ends of insatiable desire. Israel offered worship to Moloch in a vile act of child sacrifice; Israel was a people without restraint. They would be restrained by the king of Babylon because they would not restrain themselves under the benevolent and merciful reign of God. A spiritually formed person understands and practices freedom under the restraining grace of God as God works through us all to bring about peace and to heal the world.

A spiritually formed person finds freedom under the restraining yoke, the same yoke that Jesus bore. As a human being Jesus restrained his own freedom to act for the sake of living in harmony with God. Humanity and God in one harmonious whole is a portion of the good news of God in Christ. Jesus grasped humanity and God in his thought at all times and without separation.[127]

Hope's Indomitable Struggle

Hope's indomitable struggle is the choice of life when the limits of our humanness are faced with all contradiction and the encroaching power of death. Death is a power that permeates our existence like a fabric woven with a mixture of the eternal and the perishing. However, the eternal threads of God's image are capable of sustaining the temporary if we choose faith and exercise an indomitable hope. Nonetheless, the struggle is permanent and will follow us into eternity. Here, in this world, the struggle is faced with the many sins of the ancestors that have reached beyond the grave. In the next world the struggle's power will be diminished, but the choice will remain, the choice to live with other human beings before God in a harmonious unity.

The character Job vacillates from despair to occasional glimpses of possibility (hope for a different outcome). Job is a complicated book with many lessons, and hope is a dominant motif. In the Bible (NRSV), Job declares that he has no hope and says God will kill him (Job 13:15). Truly, in the face of death, we stand defeated; we all die. It is our faith in Christ's resurrection that aids us in our struggle with death. In the dialogues of Job and his friends, we find Job's hope firmly fixed in one immovable power through one indomitable vehicle: Job refuses to accept the suffering of his life as a consequence of his iniquity.[128] The indomitable

---

[127] Although Jesus cried out that God had forsaken him upon the cross, his cry is directed to God, and in a moment of inexplicable suffering this cry of Christ depicts both indomitable faith and hope in the face of all contradiction and reason (see Psalm 22:1).

[128] Although Job is read as a sinless character, he acknowledges iniquity. Job also acknowledges that God can prove him guilty even though Job is not aware of his

nature of hope lies in Job's relentless will to speak. Although he pledges silence after God overcomes him with questions and displays of power, his silence is only momentary.[129] The dialogue continues and is revealed in the effort for human beings to live in harmony with God and one another. The struggle continues for the church to live up to the ideal. The problem is that we do not accept the struggle as enduring, and instead seek Shangri La. People who attend church often experience a sense of well-being based upon acceptance, forgiveness, and a hope for fellowship; they desire Shangri-La. The desire for a better world is good and healthy. Making an effort to experience the presence of Christ in the now by bringing heaven to earth is the challenge.

Qohelet will claim that light is sweet, and it is good for the eyes to see the sun (Ecc. 11:7). Every morning is a new day, a resurrection from the night before. Every day is rich with hope for an outcome other than the ones we worry so much about. Yet every day is filled with disappointment and, for many, often with despair. Amidst the suffering and the struggle, if you will, '*life* is sweet, and it is good to see the sun'. Life is a gift from God, and life is filled with sweetness for those who develop spiritually with faith and hope.

A Short Story on Character

Standing near a McDonalds located in the fast food section of a modern shopping mall, I observed a mother handing three neatly packaged 'Happy Meals' to three small children. The three children quickly opened their neatly packaged meals and removed the throw-away plastic toy contained within. The oldest girl, who looked to be around eight years of age, seemed displeased with her throw-away toy, and grabbed the toy of her younger sister, offering hers in exchange. The youngest of the children, observing all the activity of the older ones, also wanted the toy that the middle girl possessed. Soon there was pushing, pulling, tears, and shouts for mommy to intervene. It did not appear that any of the children were interested in the food contained in their neatly packaged 'Happy Meals.'

A few days later I was in Venezuela on the streets in the evening, and I saw three little girls, alone, with their hair unkempt and their clothes worn from continual wear. The oldest girl was standing barefoot with her finger in her mouth rubbing perhaps a sore or a tooth that needed attention. The younger girls stood

---

own guilt. Job contends that he is innocent and draws God into the courtroom of human understanding, suggesting that human beings can be judged justly only if God limit judgment to the capacities of human reason.

[129] I suggest that had the story of Job continued, the character Job would have complained about the loss of his children and the memory of his sufferings.

near their older sibling, both of them looking bewildered and frightened. The smallest girl ventured a smile as I approached them. They were standing to the side of a bakery, and it was obvious that they were hungry. They were not allowed to enter the bakery or to stand directly in front of it. There was some commotion as I brought the three little girls with me into the bakery. However, seeing I was an American with money, the people working in the bakery decided not to protest my activity. I allowed each girl to pick a couple of items from the glass display. I had each of the girl's food placed into a single brown paper bag. After paying for the food I walked outside and gave each girl her own little sack of food. The older girl led her younger siblings carefully across the street. The street was like a thousand others in oppressed nations; it was busy, filled with vehicles that do not stop for pedestrians. Upon arrival to the other side, I watched as the oldest sister motioned for six other girls to join them. Soon there were nine happy little girls, giggling and playing and sharing three small sacks of bakery goods. The simplicity of friends and food overcame fear and hunger.

I have seen this story re-enacted across the world. Most readers will be thinking about the character of the girls faced with the struggle of life and not about the spoiled children of the fast food world. Spiritual formation is portrayed through the development of character. We all enter the body of Christ from numerous experiences and formed behaviors, and we are all in need of God's work to bring us into the world as new creations who are 'being saved.'

The community in which the poor girls lived had instilled within them a character that surpassed the children of consumer culture. The development of character is consistent with spiritual formation, and this story indicates that a wide array of factors contribute to the development of a person's character.

An Alternative Community

When a community of believers is birthed, the desire of God is to form an educational and living environment for the development of character; character development contributes to spiritual growth and formation. The biblical narratives all have in common a single theme. God speaks and longs for us to listen and obey. The biblical refrain "Today if you will hear his voice" has perennial ramifications because every day is today. Although God speaks every day, it seems culture, religious dogmas, and a host of other factors impede or stifle our ability to hear. Jesus repeatedly uses the phrase, "Let anyone with ears to hear listen.'"

An alternative community's task is to form a cultural living environment within a larger culture. The formed living environment is to facilitate the ability of people living under its influence to hear the voice of God, which is to discern what the Spirit is saying today. The many voices hearing God are subject to a dialogue where the word and the exemplars within the community aid in discerning direction for the community. Every Christian community has its particular distinctive that identifies hopes and intent for impacting the culture within which they exist.

In pursuit of sharing themselves within the larger culture, life continues on for the members of the community. Life is always challenging and the addition of Christian service organized for fulfilling hopes to impact the larger culture further complicates life. This is so because the existing cultural powers which dominate the national symbols of education, government, and media, also have the power to conscript our children into military service. The alternative community is an aggressive but cooperative community that cannot be conformed to the dominant systems of any society. The church and the state can never be bedfellows. The reign of God is not consistent with any existing form of government.

Learning to be human seems to be the more immediate task at hand, and yet within this formative task we pursue sharing our journey with others through acts of kindness and an active witness that is visible to the surrounding culture. There is no arrival point; there is only the journey, the struggle.[130]

God in Christ became a human being without exception and exemplified spiritual maturation as a human being, limited to his moment in history, restrained by his cultural identity, subject to the dominate powers of Rome, and his uniqueness as the Son of God. The work of the Holy Spirit is to conform people to the image of God in Christ. We have exalted Jesus (rightly so), yet we have not listened to the simplicity of our task. It is not to become more than human; it is to become completely formed as a human being. It is an obtainable goal relative to the immediate moment and requires constant challenge.

> Somewhere between Joy and Sorrow
> Amidst Laughter and Tears
> Life's Struggle is Overcome in Simplicity's Smile
>
> by Mike Garner

---

[130] Paul the apostle understood the journey, the struggle, and acknowledged that in spite of all the grace that had overtaken him, he had not arrived at an endpoint, nor does he make the endpoint obtainable in the present.

BIBLIOGRAPHY

Anderson, Robert M. *Vision of the Disinherited*. Peabody, MA: Hendrickson Publishers, 1979.

Appleby, Scott R. *The Ambivalence of the Sacred*. Oxford: Rowman and Littlefield, 2000.

Badiou, Alan. *Saint Paul: The Foundation of Universalism*. Palo Alto, CA: Stanford University Press, 2003.

Beckham, William. *The Second Reformation: Reshaping the Church for the 21st Century*. Touch Outreach Ministries: Touch Publications, 1995.

Bellinger, Charles K. *The Genealogy of Violence: Reflections on Creation, Freedom, and Evil*. New York: Oxford University Press, 2001.

Botterweck, G. Johannes, and Helmer Ringgren, eds. *Theological Dictionary of the Old Testament*. Translated by John T. Willis. Grand Rapids, MI: Eerdmans, 1974.

Boyles, Craig. *The Conflict of Faith and Experience in the Psalms: A Form Critical and Theological Study*. London: Sheffield Academic Press, 1988.

Brock, Rita Nakashima, and Susan Brooks Thistlethwaite. *Casting Stones: Prostitution and Liberation in Asia and the United States*. Minneapolis, MN: Fortress Press, 1996.

Brook, Wes Howard, and Anthony Gwyer. *Unveiling Empire: Revelation Then and Now*. Maryknoll, NY: Orbis Books, 1999.

Brown, Raymond E. *An Introduction to the New Testament*. New York: Doubleday, 1997.

Burke, Kevin F., and Robert Lassalle-Klein, eds. *Love that Produces Hope: The Thought of Igancio Ellacuria*. Collegeville, MN: Liturgical Press, 2006.

Carter, Craig A. *Rethinking Christ and Culture: A Post-Christendom Perspective.* Grand Rapids, MI: Brazos Press, 2006.

—. *The Politics of the Cross: The Theology and Social Ethics of John Howard Yoder.* Grand Rapids, MI: Brazos Press, 2001.

Chardin, Pierre Teilhard de. *The Pehnomenon of Man.* Translated by Bernard Wall. New York: Harper Collins, 2002.

Cullen, Shay. *Passion and Power.* Mulligar, Ireland: Killynon House Books, 2006.

Dunning, Stephen N. *Dialectical Readings: Three Types of Interpretation.* University Park, PA: Pennsylvania State University Press, 1997.

Easterly, William. *The White Man's Burden.* New York: Penguin Press, 2006.

Ellul, Jacques. *Money and Power.* Basingstoke, England: InterVarsity Press, 1984.

—. *The Meaning of the City.* Grand Rapids, MI: Eerdmans, 1970.

—. *The Technological Society.* New York: Knopf/Vintage, 1967.

—. *Violence: Reflections from a Christian Perspective.* London: SCM Press, 1970.

—. *Reason for Being: A Meditation on Ecclesiastes.* Grand Rapids, MI: Eerdmans, 1990.

Enloe, Cynthia. *Bananas, Beaches and Bases: Making Feminist Sense of International Politics.* Berkley and Los Angeles: University of California Press, 1990.

Freedman, David Noel, ed. *The Anchor Bible Dictionary.* 6 vols. Grand Rapids, MI: Eerdmans, 1992.

Freire, Paulo. *Pedagagy of Freedom: Ethics, Democracy and Civic Courage.* Translated by Patrick Clarke. Lanham, MD: Rowman and Littlefield Publishers, 1998.

—. *Pedagogy of the Oppressed.* Translated by Myra Bergman Ramos. New York: Continuum International Publishing Group, Inc., 2005.

Gay, Craig M. *Cash Values: Money and the Erosion of Meaning in Today's Society.* Grand Rapids, MI: Eerdmans, 2004.

Girard, Rene. *I See Satan Fall Like Lightning.* Translated by James G. Williams. Maryknoll, NY: Orbis Books, 2001.

—. *Things Hidden Since the Foundation of the World.* Translated by Stephen Bann and Michael Metteer. Palo Alto, CA: Stanford University Press, 1978.

—. *Violence and the Sacred.* Translated by Patrick Gregory. Baltimore, MD: The Johns Hopkins University Press, 1979.

Grody, Daniel G. *Globalization, Spirituality, and Justice.* Maryknoll, NY: Orbis Books, 2007.

Gunkel, Hermann. *Water for a Thirsty Land.* Minneapolis, MN: Augsburg Fortress, 2001.

Gutierrez, Gustavo. *A Theology of Liberation.* Maryknoll, NY: Orbis Books, 1973.

Hauwerwas, Stanley. *The Peaceable Kingdom.* Notre Dame, IN: University of Notre Dame, 1983.

Holladay, William L. *Jeremiah 1 Hermeneia (Hermeneia: A Critical & Historical Commentary on the Bible),* Philadelphia: Augsburg Fortress Press, 1986.

Hunter, James Davison. *To Change the World: The Irony, Tragedy, and Possibility of Christianity in the Late Modern World.* Oxford, NY: Oxford University Press, 2010.

Kaufmann, Yehezkel. *The Religion of Israel from its Beginnings to the Babylonian Exile.* Trans. by Moshe Greenberg New York: Shocken Books, 1960.

Kierkegaard, Søren, Reidar Thomte, and Albert Anderson. *The concept of anxiety: a simple psychologically orienting deliberation on the dogmatic issue of hereditary sin.* Princeton, N.J.: Princeton University Press, 1980.

—. *The Book on Adler.* Translated by Howard V. Hong and Edna Hong. Princeton, NJ: Princeton University Press, 1998.

—. *The Sickness Unto Death.* Translated by Howard V. Hong and Edna Hong. Princeton, NJ: Princeton University Press, 1980.

—. *Practice In Christianity.* Translated by Howard V. Hong and Edna Hong. Princeton, NJ: Princeton University Press, 1991.

—. *Eighteen Upbuilding Discourses.* Translated by Howard V. Hong and Edna Hong. Princeton, NJ: Princeton University Press, 1990.

—. *Without Authority.* Translated by Howard V. Hong and Edna Hong. Princeton, NJ: Princeton University Press, 1997.

Ott, Craig, and Harold A. Nerland, eds. *Globalizing Theology: Belief and Practice in an Era of World Christianity.* Grand Rapids, MI: Baker Academic, 2006.

Peterson, Eugene H. *The Jesus Way: A Conversation On The Way That Jesus Is The Way.* Grand Rapids, MI: Eerdmans, 2007.

Ramachandra, Vinoth. *Subverting Global Myths.* Downers Grove, IL: IVP Academic Press, 2008.

Ricoeur, Paul. *Time and Narrative, Volume 1.* Translated by Kathleen McLaughlin and David Pellauer. Chicago: University of Chicago Press, 1984.

Shiva, Vandana. *Earth Democracy: Justice, Sustainability, and Peace.* Brooklyn, NY: South End Press, 2005.

Sobrino, Jon. *Where is God? Earthquake, Terrorism, Barbarity, and Hope.* Maryknoll, NY: Orbis Books, 2004.

—. *No Salvation Outside the Poor: Prophetic Utopian Essays.* Maryknoll, NY: Orbis Books, 2008.

—. *Witnessses fo the Kingdom: The Martyrs of El Salvador and the Crucified Peoples.* Maryknoll, NY: Orbis Books, 2003.

Stassen, Glen H., and David P. Gushee. *Kingdom Ethics: Following Jesus in Contemporary Context.* Downers Grove, IL: InterVarsity Press, 2003.

Suchocki, Marjorie Hewitt. *The Fall to Violence: Original Sin in Relational Theology.* New York: The Continuum International Publishing Group, Inc., 2004.

Tillich, Paul. *The Courage To Be.* London: Yale University Press, 1980.

Volf, Miroslav. *Exclusion and Embrace: A Theological Exploration of Identity, Otherness, and Reconciliation.* Nashville, TN: Abingdon Press, 1996.

Weaver, Denny J. *The Nonviolent Atonement.* Grand Rapids, MI: Eerdmans, 2001.

Willard, Dallas. *Knowing Christ Today: Why We Can Trust Spiritual Knowledge.* New York: Harper Collins, 2009.

Wink, Walter. *Engaging the Powers.* Minneapolis, MN: Augsburg Fortress Press, 1992.

Yoder, John Howard. *The Politics of Jesus.* Grand Rapids, MI: Eerdmans, 1972.

Zinn, Howard. *A People's History of the United States.* New York: Harper Collins, 2003.

www.ingramcontent.com/pod-product-compliance
Lightning Source LLC
Chambersburg PA
CBHW071449160426
43195CB00013B/2061